CW01080781

Understand Your Truth
to Find Success

by Gillie Barlow

Copyright

Understand Your Truth to find Success
bringing out the best in you

First Edition 2018
Copyright © 2018 Gillie Barlow

There are two ways copyright applies to this book. Feel free to ascribe to the one that you prefer. They both work, but in different worlds. (Optional)

The New Way
If you by chance come across a copy of this book without paying for it, buy a copy and gift it to someone else. All reviews also help to keep things spinning. Good ones make an author's day. Not so good ones help authors improve their writing. This all helps to keep everything in balance.

The Traditional View
All rights reserved. No part of this publication may be reproduced, stored in or introduced into a retrieval system, or transmitted, in any form, or by any means (electronic, mechanical, photocopying, recording, or otherwise) without the prior written permission of the publisher. This book is sold subject to the condition that it shall not, by way of trade or otherwise, be lent, resold, hired out, or otherwise circulated without the publisher's prior consent in any form of binding or cover other than that in which it is published and without a similar condition including this condition being imposed on the subsequent purchaser.

Cover image : ©

Dedication

For my amazing 3 boys Ben, Josh and Jacob who I love above and beyond. That you may know your worth and understand fully the gift of love and life.

Foreword

"Sarah, don't look at me when we walk in or I'll laugh," I said.

"Come in," commanded the deputy head.

My twin Sarah and I had been summoned to the deputy head's office after a report that we had been talking 'telepathically' across the classroom and copying each other's work.

School was not the most productive place for identical twins who preferred adventure to studying and caused immense frustration to teachers who hated not knowing one from the other.

"Look at me when I am talking to you," he said sternly.

We raised our heads and, with just a glimpse of each other from the corner of our eyes, Sarah and I exploded with laughter. This didn't go down well.

Seriously angry and humiliated, the deputy head ordered me out of the room and proceeded to slam Sarah with lies about the person she was. This was our life at school.

At times it may have seemed funny, but the negativity, condemnation, and frustration, which we seemed to cause simply by being ourselves, was nothing to laugh about. It was detrimental to the core.

Even as identical twins, we were – and still are – individuals with our own DNA, our own characters, our own lives, our own passions and desires, our own gifts and our own purposes.

With well over seven billion people on our planet, this raises several questions:

How do we feel as one of so many?

How easy is it to feel insignificant ?

Why do so many people not realise their value?

So this book is about you, your worth and your value.

It's also an exploration of why your uniqueness is so truly wonderful and it leads you to discover the joy of knowing your reason-to-be.

Chapter 1 : Looking at You

Do you ever wake up in the morning and think to yourself that 'I am the only person who is me. I am the only person who will ever truly know me as I know me, and no one else will ever be me'?

If, like me, you find yourself thinking about that, how does it make you feel? Excited, relieved for others—or perhaps desperate for yourself?

It is time for you to become excited about who you are and who you have been made to be, to know an inner contentment and comprehend what a life of fulfilment can mean.

In order to do that, you will need to take yourself out of your immediate situation and predicaments, closing your eyes to everything outside of who you are. The reason for this is that those things exterior to you— such as work, people, projects, pressures, family, money, and health—are possibly shaping who you are right now and it is time to make *them* the result of *you*.

You need to be working from the inside out. This is powerful, and understanding it will take you on a journey that will lead you to be and to achieve what you aspire to and desire in your heart.

If you find contentment first, how much more are you going to achieve? Your attitude will then come from a completely different space. You will no longer feel the need to achieve in order to find happiness and contentment; that will come from your core—the person that you are.

Picture an apple. A whole apple has a core within it. If the core is bad, perhaps   with a worm or two, will it taste good? Will it look as rosy and crisp? No it won't—the apple will taste as bad as the core is rotten! In the same way, if the apple core is wonderfully healthy and untouched, the apple is going to be healthy from the inside out.

So here's a big question:

If you were that apple, how would you look? How would you taste?

I wonder where you are right now with your thoughts? Are you about to become busy and not have time to listen? Are you going to carry on doing things the way you are because it means not having to deal with what's inside you?

Is it OK with you if we park fear for a while? This is choice, my friend. People spend years trying to find contentment in all the wrong places and often never find it. Life is a gift, as are you. It is too precious—as are you—to be wasted.

So, now that fear is out of the way, let's explore how to find contentment, and make this life everything that you have dreamed it could be—and more.

I was 22 years old and struggling at work due to some unpleasantness that wafted around like a bad smell. I chose to go and speak with a couple who were recommended to me as counsellors. What they helped me understand was that, although lies had been told about me, there was probably also an element of truth in what had been said.

In other words, I was at fault as well. Although I had never believed myself to be perfect, facing the truth about my imperfections was difficult, especially when presented to me by people who didn't really know me. I could have shrugged their wise words off but I made a choice from that day on to be as aware as possible of my shortcomings, to log them, deal with them, accept them, and grow out of them.

Of course, I don't always manage to do that, but the message I absorbed that day was that I would need to work on myself to become more whole. This was an active choice I made because I knew that I was, and still am, a work in progress.

Imagine a flower. Does the bud come first, or the petal? You wouldn't find a flower without a bud. Now, in the place of the petals, put everything in your life that is exterior to you. As with the petals they should not come first. The petals are the result of the bud, just as you, and everything exterior to you in your life, should come out of who you are.

Now imagine that the bud is still forming, so there are no petals yet, which means hopefully that everything exterior to you can be set aside for the time being. That isn't easy I know, but in order to address your core and become centred you are going to need some 'you' time. How that might look is up to you. Reflection, meditation, and undisturbed moments of contemplation are just some ways in which people look inward. Devoting time to looking inward is something you need to do regularly in order to start living 'the right way in'. This may initially seem alien and maybe even annoying, and if it does, then commitment is crucial. So book some *'you'* time in your diary.

By finding this contentment within, you will stop striving and start living. I am sure that most of us strive daily, allowing pressures from those exterior areas to control our moods, emotions, and decisions. I am not saying that what I share with you in this book will stop problems, heartaches, and difficult times but if you find a place of inner contentment. Without the need for anything else, you will be able to deal with these issues from a stronger and deeper place.

Taking Back Control

Do you feel in control of your life? Or are things in your life controlling you and how you feel? What is it all about if we allow this to continue? If you continue to live the 'wrong way in' and not from the 'inside out', life may continue to be exhausting and even futile. You could miss your purpose and never tap into your gifts.

What is life all about for you? What are your priorities, your dreams, your loves, your aspirations? Do you have goals, or are you simply living to survive from one day to the next, fighting to keep your head above water? Perhaps you already have your head above the water but you feel the need to be better than the next person all the time, desperately striving to be noticed and recognised.

Do you have time to enjoy life – I mean to really enjoy life? Do you notice the beauty around you? Are you allowing yourself to be controlled or are you trying to control things that you can't?

Close your eyes and take a deep breath and trust that those battles you are fighting that sap your energy will disappear. Trust that the feeling of hopelessness and the grasping at straws to survive or stay sane will fade, and the erratic emotions you experience from day to day will stabilise.

It's easy to feel satisfied when everything is working exactly the way you planned it, but in life, in business, and in our deepest places how often does that happen? If you allow the things that are outside of *who* you are to dictate *how* you are, you become a puppet on a string – and all for what? For materialism, or for shallow and often fickle happiness?

No, you no longer have to achieve to find happiness and contentment as *this* will come from your core.

Are you setting out on this journey fearful that you won't get what you desire? That's OK, I just want you to imagine your flower with no petals – no predicaments, no other people to consider or work to get done, no food to prepare or children to look after, no money to worry about or bills to pay, no person to confront, or bridge to cross, no boss to please or target to meet, no sick person to look after or commute to make. No petals, just the bud. Just you.

Know that finding contentment requires heart and mind shifts, but not monumental learning that takes years to grasp.

I remember driving down Oxford's Botley Road in 1991 on my way to work. I was employed by a company developing risk analysis software and I had got myself the job by talking my way in. Having left school at 16 with no qualifications, my mouth was my only means of getting the jobs I wanted. Needless to say, when the alarm clock went off each day during the first month I became an instant nervous wreck because it terrified me to step into an environment I didn't understand, to be around people who didn't speak my language (and by that I don't mean English, but techie jargon), and to be selling a product that I couldn't even spell. As I drove in, I wished to be wise and capable where I felt anything but. It was some years later that it dawned on me that, with determination and a right attitude, I had become more capable from the moment I decided to, and that it hadn't and didn't need to take a long time.

In the same way, that heart and mind shift to find contentment starts when you decide that you want it to.

Think of a snowball. The centre of that snowball is clean and pure, white as white. It represents you, before you were moulded by your experiences, both good and bad. As the tiny snowball rolls in the garden it gets bigger and bigger; this represents your journey through life. On the way, the snowball picks up rubbish and dirt, especially as the snow on the ground thins and the mud shows through. So too on your journey you will have picked up rubbish – perhaps lies, hurt, pain, distortion of truth, loneliness, emptiness or abandonment. Taking time to identify and remove those thorns, stones, mud, and leaves from the snowball will start to make it white again, making you more whole for every one that is removed.

To do this you need to give thought to why you feel the way you do and look at your priorities. This means being kind to yourself. It's time to create a centred you and stable ground with a solid foundation on which to build your life and your future. That foundation is a peaceful, content, courageous, and determined you.

New Beginnings

That, my friend, is where we begin.

You have a responsibility in this life to make the most you can of it, and your happiness is entirely up to you. The time we have here is just a flicker. It burns hot and then it's gone. You may struggle with that but it is a truth you need to start accepting. Life is such a privilege, and beginning each day with gratitude will trigger the change instantly. Your purpose is unique; it's yours and no one else's, and it's one that you should be passionate about. You may know already deep down what your purpose is or what you would like it to be. You may be running from what you believe it is because you are fearful, or you may have no idea at the moment what your purpose is. Whatever it is, I can guarantee that if you want to know fulfilment and make the most of the privileged life you have, coming from a place of contentment you will be passionate inside your purpose. You will smile enormously and your enthusiasm will draw people to you.

Let's return to the flower. Imagine now you have picked some petals and put them neatly on the table in the shape of a flower but not touching. In the centre there is nothing – a big gap. Those petals are everything in your life. I suggest that you take some time to list all those things.

Your list may look something like this:
Husband or wife, children, health, work, hobbies such as sport and music, travelling, money, goals, any other relationships, dreams, pressures, cars, holidays.

These are all petals in their different ways. Your life will be transformed – whether you are already in a good place right now, an OK place, or a bad place – if you let your contentment be found first in *you*, and not in the petals on your list.

Let's look briefly at what may be on your list. Work is possibly part of your life, and you may gain great satisfaction from it, and be growing significantly in terms of your ability and confidence. Alternatively, it may be a place that you feel terrorised on entering, or drained of all energy, or manipulated and controlled, or maybe it just seems a road to nowhere. Whatever it might be to you, if it is making you what you are today, perhaps it has come as a 'petal' before the bud – the 'strived-for result' before contentment. Is busyness preventing enjoyment, is pressure resulting in ill health, or is the desperation for money giving you cause to believe you will never get there?

A few years ago a friend came to me for some advice. Divorced with children and remarried, he was travelling weekly in a high-pressured job where he was paid for eight hours, expected to work for twelve and controlled for twenty-four. He had become depressed and was struggling to find purpose. His life was now merely about survival. He was rarely getting time to see the people he loved, and when he did see them he was in a depressed state of mind. He was on a road to nowhere, and contentment and happiness were just words that didn't form part of his world.

Thankfully, at one of those crossroads (that many of us have experienced), he was able to find the courage to take back the reins of his life by coming to understand the art of living from the 'inside out'.

If health is on your list, listen up. Irrespective of why we become ill, I do believe that often how likely we are to get it and how quickly it is likely to go is enormously down to attitude. So if contentment comes before any stresses, struggles, and pressures, there is a lesser likelihood of ill health being an issue. If our attitude has a 'high altitude' we will also be on top of keeping fit, respecting our bodies, and looking after them. Lack of exercise and fitness can cause lethargy and apathy, which in itself can cause demotivation and even depression.

I remember when I used to speak regularly in prison, making every effort to get eye contact with some of the guys, in order to engage with them as I spoke. This wasn't just because I wanted them to understand the message, but because so many of them were on anti-depressants which made them drowsy and more likely to drift off in the warmth of the chapel.

It is no different when you don't take care of yourself; lethargy sets in and opportunity can pass you by, as can life. Exercise and being active releases endorphins which help mental wellbeing. If you are sitting feeling frustrated because you know there is truth in that, bear with me because this will all change when other things in life come second to you.

So how about sleep? How much does sleep or the lack of it affect your life, your mood, your ability to do a good job and be happy? How much does it affect your attitude and your ability to smile – or not? Sleep deprivation is a problem that is growing increasingly worse in our society. No matter what we do for a living, lack of sleep affects our day-to-day performance at work and our relationships with others around us. The physical and mental problems caused by lack of sleep are even scarier and include weight gain, memory problems, inability to perform, depression, increased cancer risk, and even the build-up of proteins in the brain associated with age-related dementia.

If you are able to live your life starting from within you, you will find that these areas take care of themselves because your attitude, your energy, and your purpose will be coming from a different space.
So the petals can now be something to look forward to, and that beginning starts with you – the only you who exists. When you have found contentment in you and you alone, you will see the privilege it is to be given the gift and the opportunity to be *you*, and you will want to be the best you can be. With renewed strength of character, because of self-belief and self-worth, you will be able to close your ears to negativity and lies and stride forward with passion and determination.

Taking Time Out

I mentioned earlier some ways in which you might take time to start looking at who you have become and how that feels. Meditation is a good way to stabilise your mind and create relaxation. It has a way of revealing compassion and wisdom but ultimately it puts you in a place where you are still.

Some years ago I discovered the wonder of deer trekking. A friend and I would go to a local wood very early in the morning with a ball of string, and tie the string to the gate where we entered, unrolling it as we walked. We had learned only too quickly that woods are easy to get lost in. We would walk slowly and as quietly as we could. Often when we reached a crossroads in the trees we would turn our heads to see deer looking straight back at us. We would be so still as we observed them and they us. Sitting on a fallen tree with the early morning dew at my feet, I discovered that dawn was magical. I will treasure those quiet moments.

To be still is so good.

Back in 1987, after I had returned from a trip with my parents and three sisters to Kenya, I spent some time at Lee Abbey, a retreat house in Devon. It was a working party week, and we were predominantly involved in physical work, helping on the estate grounds, which I loved. On one occasion I was in a team cutting back bramble bushes, which I chose because it sounded quite tame. You guessed it – it was far from tame and any bare skin at the end of the week looked like it had gone through a shredder.

On another occasion, I was in a team moving soil, which again seemed relatively tame when I saw it on the list of activities. Little did I know we would be taking it in wheelbarrows down a steep slope, and that it would rain most days. My most vivid memory is desperately trying to keep hold of a very heavy load whilst slipping on my backside down a mudslide.

Whilst in Kenya I had been offered the opportunity to fly back out to Africa, setting off again three weeks after our return to England. Not to Kenya this time but to the Kalahari Desert in Botswana. I had no job back home and knew that it was an opportunity of a lifetime. But I was also very young, would be flying 5,000 miles away from the people I knew and loved to a land that was vast in its emptiness, a culture I knew little to nothing about and into a world where I knew only one person.

I knew that at Lee Abbey I would need to do a lot of thinking, and gaining of counsel. I was fighting in my spirit as I wanted to be brave enough to go but knew it would be easy to decline and soon everyone would forget about it. My parents had both been born and brought up in Africa and lived there into their adult years. They had talked of Africa much during my childhood, and I had loved what I had seen, smelled, felt and touched of it when in Kenya. I tried in my mind to push away the truth that such an experience could significantly change me, grow me, and enrich my young life.

Within the beautiful building at Lee Abbey, up the wide oak staircase, was a small, unobtrusive chapel. Between 5 and 6 p.m. there was an opportunity to go to what was called 'A Time of Quiet'. The lights would be very low, gentle music would be playing quietly, and a picture would be projected up on a screen. I remember one evening it was a field of flowers. This was a time to sit and be, to contemplate, to be quiet, it was time for me. Even in those moments at Lee Abbey, when I was so young, I needed to be content within myself, and be sure that that came first in order to get the most out of whatever might come next.

It is important to know that 'you time' can happen anywhere. Many a time I have been coming up a button lift on a ski slope, thankful for the staggeringly beautiful place I found myself in, contemplative of my life whilst praying for the safety of my three boys who I knew would be cutting mercilessly into the slopes as they flew down at unspeakable speed.

For you, the key may be to find a place alone to reflect, to think. Time away near the sea or in the mountains, by a quiet stream or on a good walk. You probably know where you need to be, and what place and space allows you to look at what's put you where you are today.

Wherever that place is, over the next few chapters I would like to help you come to know contentment in a place deep within you – a place where only you can go, but where, quite possibly, you've not yet been.

Chapter 2 : Eliminating the Lies

If I were to ask you on a scale of one to ten what you thought of yourself, I wonder what you would honestly say?

How we feel about ourselves is largely dictated by the way we have been made to feel as we have grown up. Just like everyone else, your subconscious mind will have stored information told to you – both good and bad – which sits there until you use it, either to grow yourself or knock yourself.

It is these different pieces of information which you now need to unfold in order to illuminate the lies that you may have absorbed. By doing this you can start living a new way, a true way, a way that help you see life as the gift you have been told it is, but have possibly not yet believed it to be.

It's time to uncover every false belief and lie that's been holding you back from your new life of possibility.

Take some time to write down every single negative thing that you say or think about yourself. Sometimes we don't always realise that some thoughts are negative. One way to check is by determining whether or not they are positive. They can only be one or the other, so if it doesn't fall into the positive camp, it is a negative thought. Take as much time as you need because this is important. These could be words said once that impacted you terribly, or possibly the same words said again and again over many years. Often we genuinely believe these to be true.

A friend now living in Australia told me how, as a child growing up, they were told they were the worst person in the world. They were never allowed out and, having never lived with another family, they had nothing to compare themselves with and so had no reason to believe it wasn't true.

There are many examples of lies spoken over people of all ages that have been stored away in their subconscious minds and believed.

We can pick up some of these lies at school and can be convinced that we no ability academically or that we haven't got a musical bone in our body and can't draw to save our life. Some people can leave school with the notion that they will never amount to anything and that they are a liability and will never succeed. What sort of start in life is that?

At work we can be lead to think we promise results but never achieve them and that way we communicate with others is rubbish. We can end up thinking that we have little or nothing to offer society or the world as a whole or that we are a joke or just trouble and should be locked away.

Our partners can unwittingly tell us that we look a mess and don't know how to dress or that we are overweight and an embarrassment. Stay at home mums or dads can come quickly to the conclusion that we are a pain and just cost money.
It's time now to stop allowing others from the past or present from heaping lies and unbelief in toxic drifts across your life.

The Seeds of Lies

You now have a list of the lies that you have stored up, which have until now affected your journey. Determine where they came from and for how long you have allowed them to warp how you feel about yourself. People are very quick to recognise each other's faults but also quick to reflect their issues on to others. This could well have been behind some of the lies spoken to you.

I left school at 16, having struggled academically. The teachers found it difficult to cope with Sarah and me being so alike, being identical twins. Just days before I left school forever, a teacher came up to me and said, "You may as well go and jump off a bridge as you are going nowhere."

I was stunned into silence, which as many would tell you, is a rare thing. How did that affect me on reflection? I believe it actually fired me up to prove them wrong, and my determination helped me to step out of that place of darkness quickly, so as not to be consumed early on by lies about my value. Sadly, that has not been the case for everyone spoken to like that. Some of the lads responded in a fairly uncouth fashion; they may have been hard and loud on the outside but the condemnation and lies were absorbed and stored in their subconscious minds and they went on to do little or nothing because they were fighting their worth.

I used to think that 'Grace' was just a beautiful name for a child but I have discovered that it is so much more. It is the lens through which we should see each other, although we cannot control the 'we', only the 'I'.

21

Grace allows you to look beyond the issues of the past and the lies which you have now determined and is a key part of the training of the mind and the heart.

About 25 years ago, I met a friend who had been brought up in a loving family. She was very laid back and not a great thinker. We went away for a weekend to Cornwall and I took a guitar. I love music and take it with me whenever I can. Rachel picked up the guitar and strummed aimlessly. She said how she would love to be able to play and I told her she absolutely could if she wanted to. I showed her some chords and within five weeks she was having guitar lessons and loving it. I asked why she had never played before if she had always wanted to, and she said that at the age of seven she had taken up the violin only to be told by her teacher that she didn't have a musical bone in her body. Rachel hadn't realised until then that that one negative comment, that lie, had stopped her playing music for 24 years.

Some of the things you have taken on board may seem insignificant and small but every one you have directly or indirectly, consciously or subconsciously, responded to. By letting it shape your life, what you do, and how you think about yourself, you have accepted it as truth. You need to understand the negative impact, however significant or insignificant, that each one has had on your life. What have the lies you have carried stopped you from doing? And what have they meant you have done?

Doors will Open

Joseph Campbell once said, 'Follow your bliss and the universe will open doors for you where there were only walls.'

There is so much truth in his words. Doors really do open up before you when you make a choice to illuminate the lies and follow your bliss. But what has caused your walls to form in the first place?

I am a fairly strong character but for many years I allowed words to crush me in the moment and quietly erode the person I was. I would lie down and cry, curling into a tight ball of pain, devastated by my inability to please, to get it right, to step up to the mark, to be accepted, to be cherished. The picture that always came to mind was a large khaki-coloured army truck driving over me in deep mud. I would eventually get up and be fine all over again. I was listening to lies and, although I knew I was being hurt at the time, I didn't believe for one moment that the words were affecting the actual person I was.

Lies held me back, and the bombardment of untruths left me lost in a cloud where it seemed there was too much rain.

Now – as I am sure you do – I want to stand tall. The only thing to do therefore is to get out of the cloud, and that has to be a choice. I hear people talking so much about freedom and their desire to find it, but I want you to understand that freedom is quite simple, and readily available for you right now. It is merely choice.

Now take a look at all the negative thoughts and words you wrote down about yourself and write down the opposite. These are the statements you need to start speaking out. Illuminating lies only gives room for growth if you start to speak out truth. It opens up your world as you start to believe in yourself, that you do have purpose and gifts and can know fulfilment.

We can kill our dreams by listening to others or that small voice in our heads that tells us that we can't or we shouldn't, perhaps that we aren't worthy, or that it's above our station.

In 1988, I went skiing with a group of friends including my parents and two of my sisters. One day I decided not to go on to the slopes and visited an estate agent. I was 21 years old, looking fourteen, and spoke little to no French. As it happened, they were perfectly pleasant and seemed to take me seriously. I was found later by some of the group in a café with my Filofax, scribbling down some notes. They chuckled and said, "What are you doing? There is no way you can buy a place in a ski resort!" The truth was, on an £8,000 salary gutting fish in a fish farm, I couldn't afford the door of a chalet, let alone a whole property in a ski resort.

Had I listened to my friends and accepted what they said I would not have purchased the chalet or set up SADA (Sophia's Alpine Disabled Adventures), a charity that builds confidence up in disabled children through sports and adventure. I have seen lives touched powerfully and grown personally so much because of the journey I took in buying it and then using it for good.

As Henry Ford said, 'Whether you think you can or whether you think you can't, you're right.'

It's time to start speaking out what you want your happiness, your future, your abilities, your achievements, and your life to be. The mind is everything: what you think, you become.

Forgive and Forget

Now that you have identified the lies that have been holding you back, and maybe even where they came from, you may want to do something practical to get rid of them. This can be very powerful, so don't assume it isn't a necessity.

At Lee Abbey, the house in Devon, groups of us used to take an evening walk along the cliff edge of the estate. It was lined by trees and ended at a point known as Jenny's Leap. We would write down everything we wanted to and needed to let go of like past pain, unforgiveness or those lies we told ourselves. We would attach the note to a stone and chuck it as far as we could with a sign saying 'NO fishing'. I remember the relief, the joy, because in doing something physical it genuinely felt that from that moment life could start again.

Another way might be to burn the list of lies. Find a practical way to say 'I will not be subjected to these lies any longer. They will not be part of who I am or the direction in which my life goes.'

All those lies were told to you by people you know and one day those people – the ones who put you down, made you feel worthless, and didn't believe in you – will be the ones telling everyone how they met you.

Some of the lies that have until now defined how you think of yourself and the way in which you live may well not have come from others, but from comparisons you have made with others regarding such things as abilities, results, personality and looks. Perhaps your brother, sister, cousin, or friend. This is a form of self-annihilation and can only send you into a downward spiral. Contentment will never be found there, only bitterness, envy, jealousy, and anger, and the occasional pity party.

Whether they are lies heaped on you by insecure, soul-destroying individuals or lies you have put upon yourself – establishing a firm foundation of self-worth and illuminating those lies will allow yourself to dream bigger and bigger. It will replace the constant questions: 'Will I impress the boss and do well enough today?', 'Am I capable of getting borrowing for a house ? 'Where am I going to sleep tonight?'

This life has got to be more than survival – it is a privilege, a gift, and is to fulfil purpose.

I understand that you may know what it is to be forgotten, to be stripped of everything that makes you you, but let me assure you that your purpose *can* be found and fulfilled and you can still make a difference. Sometimes you have to look inside your heart. The truth comes from your heart in a way that no other words can.

Today is the beginning of the rest of your life. It's time to let go of everything negative that came before, live for today, and allow yourself to dream for the future.

Even once you have identified the lies you wrote down, rejected them and started speaking truth, you may still have bruising and open wounds. If this is the case, with these may come the debilitating, life-sucking echoes of bitterness that are sometimes subtle but allow negativity to remain in force.

It is time for you to forgive those people in your life. Let them go. Forgive every boss, parent, business partner, friend, work colleague, crook, or betrayer who has ever caused you grief of any kind. Clean the slate and forgive to forget. Wipe away every name and image by saying, 'I forgive them for everything, and I wish them well.' Keep saying this each time you think of the person or situation until the negative feelings are gone. This may take days or weeks, but the negative feelings will go if you persevere. This is so important as your attitude moving forward is yours to choose, and there is little point in moving forward knowing truth about who you are if it's made up of unforgiveness and bitterness.

A colleague and friend recently shared some of her story growing up. She said, "There was a strong presence of abandonment and rejection over my life. My father had wanted a boy and never bonded with me. It felt as if I was a constant let down. Having wanted a boy, he got a girl and then the girl he got looked like a boy. It seemed that wherever I turned, I was an unwanted burden. I wasn't good at the things he wanted me to be good at and the things I might have been good at didn't interest him.

This hugely affected my self-worth and I never believed I was lovable, acceptable, and beautiful. I am learning this now by rejecting the lies of my past, and instead choosing daily to believe the fact that I am endlessly valuable. I'm not perfect and struggle often, but forgiveness has given me the freedom to redefine my worth."

She went on to say, "I have learned that we cannot erase people's decisions that have impacted us, but we can choose how much they affect our future."

You cannot change what people think of you, but you can shout words of love to the lies you believed and begin on the journey to loving yourself well.

When you start realising your worth and see the miracle that you are, you will find that, when people throw mud at you it won't stick, and they'll end up realising that they're the ones who need a bath.

Chapter 3 : Believing in You

So the lies are identified and rejected. No longer will you be subjected to them or the control they have had on the direction of your life. You are now on the correct starting block, you have chosen freedom and you have an exciting expectation, which is hope. Your future and how it will look begins now as you paint the picture of your choice, using colours and textures personal to you and you alone.

How you think of yourself is paramount. It will be what steers you: the rudder to your boat. Until you learn to love yourself, loving others is very much harder, and, in the same way, until you believe fully in yourself, success is likely to be beyond your reach.

I want therefore to challenge you right now. Go to a mirror and look at yourself. Nobody can see; it's just you and your mirrored image. Without focusing on your physical features, and removing all arrogance and pretence, tell yourself on a scale of 1-10 how much you genuinely like yourself. If your rating isn't significantly high, you need to work on it. Without self-worth and self-belief, life is a hard slog and… to what end?

If your life is grey in certain areas because you have allowed yourself to be controlled – most probably by fear – decide to bring your choice of colour into that area of your life.

Don't succumb to what you see as your 'lot'. You have one chance at this life here on earth, don't let fear – of change, of letting people down, of what people will think of you, or of failure – paralyse you and stop you from dictating how that picture is painted. If you do let fear dictate, your life will never be as it was intended. You will never know what might have been because you allowed fear to win over faith.

Fear is the substance of things not desired and has the power to destroy. It will stop you making progress and steal your quality of life. Faith is the substance of things hoped for and has the power to create.

I was speaking with a lad not long out of prison and he opened up his wallet to show me a photo. As he did I noticed a piece of card inside, it had a quote on it: 'Courage is fear prayed for'. Today, how you turn fear into courage is up to you, but one or the other is going to have the upper hand.

As you start to look at who you are and who you have been made to be, decide to live boldly. Boldness helps us to confront our fear and refuses to let that emotion rule us, so that we are no longer 'slaves' to it.

Are you flying into a gale force wind? Make the choice to soar high, just as an eagle flies and allow the strong winds of peace to blow away the doubt and fear.

Eagles are magnificent birds – to be so sure of who they are, to fly with self-belief and without fear, to command their space and be graceful, and to have respect together with freedom.

You have enormous potential but having potential is not enough unless you are willing to take a risk and step out. The word 'potential' means 'existing in possibility but not actuality' Powerful but not in use.

That, my friend, is as good as a smack in the face with a wet kipper.

People waste their potential by not developing what's inside of them. Instead of developing what they have or desire, they worry about what they don't have and all their potential goes untapped.

You could be a world changer. You could make a difference in your life and in others' lives if you develop what you have, but it takes determination and hard work to develop that potential into reality. If you want things to change, you have to make changes. What changes need to be made in you? Because these could allow you to start walking a new path even if you can't see exactly where it leads.

There may be painful issues of the past that you grapple with. Those issues may have been someone else's fault and it might not be fair that you should suffer because of what they said or what they did. But whatever the source of your pain, you don't have to spend your life mourning over something you can't do anything about. Unforgiveness eats you up from the inside. In this situation, your future has absolutely no room for your past.

Millions of people miss today because they either refuse to let go of the past or they worry about the future. Perhaps you didn't have a good start in life or business or with relationships, but with the right attitude and coming from a place of contentment, you can have a good finish.

I want to remind you again to move your focus from everything exterior to you - all the people and all the things in your life - as we look at what it is to be you. By addressing this you will come from a place where you are unaffected and content before all the other aspects of your life and the things that fill it begin.

The Choice is Yours

Right now you can choose to be what you aspire to be.

It is a choice to get rid of or totally ignore that voice in your head that says otherwise. As you work from the inside out be prepared to be nothing less than the best you can be.

A friend of mine shared with me the other day that she had known what long suffering felt like. She could have given up at so many bumps in the road but she didn't. She persevered and experienced grace, restoration, and healing. In the process she was working out her purpose and on the other side she experienced incredible blessing.

What is broken can be restored.

Sorrow can turn into joy; empty can be filled; worthless can be valued; that which is not good enough can excel; shame can fade and confidence can rise. There is a purpose and plan for you, irrespective of your past choices, upbringing, culture, treatment, and projected image of who you are. Dreams matter and something has been put inside you, like a seed, that needs to be nurtured through any pain, longsuffering, or lies regarding the person you are. Step into what has been freely given to you and start living the purpose you are here to live.

In 1993 I went to a place called Sivilai in north east Thailand, so remote I'm not sure it's on the map. A women's Christian conference was taking place at which my brother in-law Mike and sister Jane spoke in fluent Thai. I didn't understand any of it but sitting on the floor in the heat and the dust I will never forget having an insane desire to stand up and say something. 'Don't be ridiculous,' I caught myself thinking, 'what could you ever speak about?'

The urge was suppressed but the seed was planted and the unexpected feelings and desire to speak were logged in my subconscious mind until some years later. I now have a passion to speak and have had the privilege of doing so many times in the last few years. A seed was planted that day which meant I had to step out of my comfort zone and be both brave and bold. Out of it came passion, fulfilment, and a great joy which I choose to believe is what life is about.

Attitude in life is essential. Where the mind goes the man follows, which is why for every negative thought about yourself, I encourage you to think of two positive thoughts. The training of the mind is an absolute necessity.

"What are you doing?" my friend said as she laughed at me across a small café in the French Alps. "I am just working out some figures to see how I can acquire a chalet in this beautiful place," I responded.

"Don't be daft", she scoffed, "you can't afford the door of a house, let alone a house".

Having set up SADA, the charity for disabled children, in 1992, when I was later in Canada in 1994 I found myself thinking of setting up SADA2 in the stunningly beautiful land that I was in. It was again a seed sown and many years later the land was purchased and a base created to build up confidence in disabled school leavers and young adults. I know that when a disabled young adult gets on a plane to travel halfway around the world with no one they know, to live in 14 acres of woodland, they are likely to be stretching themselves out of their comfort zone. It is likely to grow them exponentially and not only open up vast opportunity but help them come to know their value and worth in a deeper way.

Your comfort zone and your need to be stretched out of it could mean visiting your neighbour rather than travelling across to Canada, because the stretch is yours. That's the exciting thing about uniqueness.

I wonder if you are content to be you? Or are you wanting something different, and in the process creating your own tensions, piling up building blocks of discontentment, making your own high rise apartments of unhappiness? Are you isolating yourself in anxiety, made all the worse when the hand of reality gives the edifice a push and you sit in the ruins, inconsolable?

Have No Regrets

Woody Allen once said, "My one regret in life is that I am not someone else."

What a devastating waste – that the gift of himself should be so rejected, and gratitude and opportunity in its fullness flung into a distant place. All that he has achieved could be the result of running after things that were not for him. You cannot force a happy ending on a story that wasn't meant to be. Equally, his true purpose may never now be determined.

I have been reminded again and again that living in a state of gratitude is the gateway to grace. It is one of the most powerful emotions. When we have had enough and just want everything to stop, we can remember there is another way. A shift in our mindset can change our entire course. Gratitude for the smallest of things on a regular basis will make differences you wouldn't believe.

You may have known pain, shame, broken relationships, illnesses, loss, financial hardship, discouragement, and hopelessness, and you may be feeling limp and weak from trying. This is why knowing who you are and feeling fantastic about it first – before any one of life's challenges face you – is the way forward. We are not on this earth to accumulate victories or trophies or experience, or even to avoid failure, but to be whittled and sandpapered down until we learn who we truly are. To be restored, regardless of our past. To allow ourselves to be who we were made to be and to be comfortable and grateful for who we are.

You have never failed until you stop trying – until you stop believing in yourself. Yes, you – the only you there will ever be. You owe it to yourself therefore to be the best you can be and that cannot and will not happen until your core of self-worth, love and self-belief gives you opportunity for inner happiness and contentment. This will allow the masks and procrastination – which is merely another word for 'tomorrow' – to disappear. It will allow the lies inside you that tell you 'you can't and you won't' to evaporate, and hope to rise in their place.

It is time to surround yourself with people who do you good and not harm. Let them lift you up when you fall and let yourself grow from it all. Faith is so important here.

I'm talking to you, no one else. You have so much to offer and it's time to stop taking the easy option, blindfolding yourself to the possibilities, that are only at an arm's reach, because it's safer to stay where you are. Tell me, if you do stay where you are, what will that feel like in five years' time? Will the painting of your life be created by you or by someone else?

When You Are Gone

Four years ago, I was part of a group where I learned a lot about the power of coaching. At the first session we were all asked to share a little of who we were and our lives to date, and then where we saw ourselves going. Three of us had stood up and spoken when Harry got up. He was 30 years old and spoke fluently. I was dumbstruck by his life, by what he had achieved and experienced, and to be honest I couldn't imagine what else he could be hoping to do. He talked about charity work that had involved creating huge irrigation systems in Africa and spoke of being part of government discussions to improve links between different nations.

It was only when he finished that the twist came: he had read to us what he hoped would be written in his eulogy. Write down now what you would like people to say you did in your life when you've gone. This is a way to start looking at your potential purpose and passion. Think about everything and anything positive in your life and thoughts – what you enjoy, what you feel you are good at or what you would like to be good at, what makes you smile and light up. Intimidation, victimisation and lies are all gone; it's time to have faith, to stand tall and make your life your own.

It's time to be good to yourself, kind to yourself, to imagine that this life is, in a magical way, supposed to be everything you would wish it to be and desire it to be. I am not talking about greed, but real heart stuff. When you have imagined that world, that place, tell me why you can't have it.

The lies are history, you are in control and have choice. The world is your oyster and you are as amazing and able as the next person. So do you want it enough?

Fear has a habit of conquering, using every rational-sounding reason under the sun to camouflage itself, but this time that's not going to happen.

How many lives are you going to change by being you? Believing in who you are and understanding that you have a purpose and are of significant value and finding that deep inner contentment will draw people to you. I honestly believe that working from the inside out you will find that how you feel and what you believe will create reactions and responses that will give you every ability to succeed in relationships and business like never before.

The Power of Welcome

It was late July in my second year of running SADA, and the sun was magnificent in the sky, the bright red geraniums ablaze in the flower troughs on the balcony, their colour stunning against the rich wood of the chalet. The disabled children and helpers were milling around after lunch, chilling, some looking for grasshoppers on the bank, and others playing quiet games after a manic morning flying down 800 metres of metal track on the luge. We had great banter with the children, telling them how they gave us such a great holiday and they would insist in return that it was we who gave them the great holiday. They never fully realised the joy they gave us through their smiles, their gratitude, their love for life, and total acceptance more often than not, of conditions which would be with them for life.

I had told them that the helper arriving midway through the week did not know anyone other than me and that a warm welcome would be great.

Marko arrived and Jenny, aged seven, stood at the top of the outside steps, with two sticks to keep her upright and thick curly hair falling onto her shoulders. She smiled a smile that I can only suggest you close your eyes to imagine and called out, "MAAARKO!" A man who hadn't cried for 15 years later admitted that tears filled his eyes in that moment. Jenny had so much to offer him and she made a stranger feel not only welcome but at home, at ease.

I will always remember that day and it will forever remind me of the value of a smile and the power it can have on others. Twenty-five years on and Jenny still has the most unbelievable smile. I wonder how many people during those years have been affected by it.

Now mentally peel away all the stuff that has collected around you and imagine all the thorns, stones, and dirt removed from your snowball, and that the 'clean, perfect you' is what you now have. Describe to yourself what that is and what it looks like. It's time to get excited about you, whittled and sand papered and taken back to just you. What's your response? You can choose excitement at what's to come, or you can choose fear. Don't allow fear to win. This is your life and yours alone – there is never a greater time than now to be bold and determined, courageous and sure. Whatever you want to do in this world, just *do it*!

Just Be You

Pressures are often put on people by others around them. Some in authority, maybe colleagues or perhaps family members, try to convince those they can of the direction they should go and how they should be. They try to control by commanding the ways others look, behave, and conduct themselves.

This comes in all forms, and some examples might be the pressure to go to university or to stay in the family business. Family pressures may lead you to conform to other people's beliefs and standards and to be responsible and make lots of money. Corporate life can lead us to dress and communicate in a certain way or to become what someone else tells us we must be.

Of course, those inner lies may surface again at any time if current events trigger old patterns. So you may become invisible because you are useless or be tempted to not be seen and heard

If you can relate to any of this, it's time to stop pushing water uphill. It's time to stop doing what you don't like because you believe you have to. If you don't stop life will pass you by at such speed, and the real you, the one you've been made to be, will never surface.

You have got to get rid of the lies and shed the unwanted control and you are getting closer to finding the untarnished, self-respecting gift that you are. I understand that even if you see what I am attempting to put across, it may seem hard if your life at the moment is difficult due to predicaments and situations. But I promise you things will start to change if you put some of what I have said into practice.

If you have got to where you are because of a series of bad decisions, overcome the results of them now by making a series of good ones. You are free to choose what you think, what you do and who you spend time with. Freedom of choice is wonderful.

I was sitting in the car with my friend some months ago. She had had a very tough time when her husband of 24 years had left. She had been told many times that she was useless and had become riddled with fear, allowing the lies to trap her in a state of paralysis. Every time she slowed down, she heard a voice saying she'd never be good enough, that she'd never be worthy of a good man.

After talking with her for a while, she went away and thought about what the best year in her life would be: how it would look, smell, and feel. She then made the brave decision to allow that year to be the picture she painted for her future – that dream. That was the beginning of the rest of her life. She had a choice to go down with the ship or to rise up and have the victory.

Your life is too precious to be compromised by anyone or anything, so make a decision that yours won't be.

I want you to imagine a big coin rolling down a hill, rather like a tyre. Now think about the times either you or others have said things like, 'When I get that job it'll all be all right', 'When I've passed the exam life will be OK', 'As soon as I make another few pounds I will be happy' or 'Once we have the bigger house life will be good.'

These are examples of people allowing things *outside* of who they are to be their source of contentment and happiness. Many spend years – maybe all their lives – before they learn the true art of contentment. If it is a financial goal you are striving for, after months or years, you will probably find your boundaries of contentment have changed and you are likely not to find it.

As the coin rolls at speed downhill, people chase after it. That is natural – we all know the phrase 'Money makes the world go round.' Money is a necessity, but it's also a chicken and egg situation. What comes first? Happiness and contentment, or money? You may be the person chasing it and you may catch it and hold it for a while but then it slips from your grasp due to the steepness of the slope and the speed at which it rolls. You don't give up though, and run after it again, catching it a second time but repeating what happened the first time – again and again and again.

Thus you end up chasing money for years, grabbing what you can when you can but always wanting more and never being satisfied. You may catch it and with all your strength keep hold of it, accumulating more, but the strain doesn't create happiness as the concentration, stress, and continued commitment to hold it leaves no time or energy to enjoy life. Or you may never catch or hold of the coin, and deem yourself hopeless.

It is quite possible that you recognise yourself in this scenario.

Embrace Don't Chase

As you look at who you are and brush off all that isn't you, don't run from suffering – embrace it. Don't chase happiness – find it first. Self-sacrifice is the only way to find yourself by stripping away what you think you need but don't. What kind of deal is it to get everything you want but lose yourself or never truly know yourself? What could you ever trade your soul for?

Much of what human beings go through is so big. We have been created to love and be loved and that, at the end of the day, is what we all want. It may be dressed up in different ways such as acceptance, support, gifts, time, words, acts of service, approval, and touch but it is what it is.

Free will is a gift, and love is a choice, hate gives a person no choice. That is why negativity in the form of pain, abandonment, abuse, and much more, is part of the lives we live. How you respond to adversity can make a huge difference to your health and your life. No matter what your situation is, life will inevitably challenge you but I do believe that by living from the inside out you will have the tools to meet those challenges. Although they may affect the person you are on the surface, they will not affect the core of who you truly are.

So if love is the reason for it all, as you look at the 'you', the bud of the flower, before life outside of you, what do you consider your attributes to be? Has your heart been hardened? Consider for a moment what you believe others to think of you, the type of person you are, your characteristics, the good, and the not so good. How do you feel you come across and is that the way you want to been seen? Who are you drawn to and why?

I would suggest that most people will be drawn to positive, warm, kind, selfless, and genuine people. The only people drawn to negative people are generally other negative people.

Selfishness is definitely a characteristic to watch out for. It is a destroyer, a keeper, a grabber, and it creates an emptiness and a futility that makes up for nothing. If this is a characteristic of yours, you need to be set free from it and be restored back to the 'you' that came before everything else. Often this comes from a place of fear. No longer let it be 'me me me' on your mind, but choose to be fruitful, to hold your head up high, have confidence, to stop going through your day afraid but choose to make somebody else's life better because of the attributes and gifts you have been given. The journey that you choose to travel now could revolutionise lives or challenge the odds. You may have no idea where it will take you but with the right attitude, self-belief, tools, authenticity, willingness, and freedom to start, it is a gift in your hands for you to take.

To find purpose in all that you may have been through and to move from struggle to freedom you need to be restored. Regardless of the past you can then be who you were made to be, and be comfortable with and grateful for the person you are.

The journey will bring you from a place of questioning your future to one of exciting purpose.

I had a picture several years ago of myself with a lead attached which someone else several feet behind me was holding. They were in a sinking bog. I tried with all my might to continue to move forward but it was a constant strain as the force of the downward pull fought against the direction I was going. I yearned to cut the lead so that I could fly like an eagle and be me – that's all I wanted to be allowed to be. The eagle is the king of birds, the most majestic and powerful winged creature on earth. It is not intimidated by heights or forceful winds that other birds might fear. It takes advantages of the gales, setting its wings so the gusts lift it higher. Eagles don't waste time battling with other birds. It is very easy to get used to being treated wrongly, to simply accept it and carry on, but it takes courage to make change happen. It is well worth it, however, when you remember this is the only life on earth that you will get, and it's your life and no one else's.

It's so easy to think that truth is simple, a matter of black and white, wrong or right. Sometimes it is and its stark simplicity challenges us to live in its light, but at other times, because of human weakness, it's much more complicated. Life can be a puzzling mixture of light and shade and dimly lit paths. It is therefore, for some, a complex issue. For others, faith involves having the courage to hang on when life is problematical. Right now, you have the choice to decide what the truth is about you.

How you feel about yourself is much more important than how anyone else feels about you.

The way you think about yourself is far more important than how anyone else thinks about you, and the way you talk about yourself is absolutely more important than the way anyone else talks about you.

Believing in who you are creates a strength of character within that stops you worrying about what other people think. It brings stability and offers a sense of assurance at all times as you live your life doing your best – which in any culture, society, predicament, or situation is all anyone can ask.

Three years ago I went to a wonderful place in western Kenya called Oyugis, where I was visiting widows and orphans cared for by a Christian charity I support. One day, we were travelling out of the town when a student asked if we could give him a lift back to college.

I have never forgotten the words on the back of his T-shirt: 'Champions don't just happen by chance. You have to choose to be one.'

Chapter 4 : Finding Your Passion

To me, success is simple – it's a 'good life'.

What a good life means to me may be completely different from what it means to you. People get confused though in thinking that success is a financial or materialistic destination, and that when it is finally reached 'the good life' begins. If success is a 'good life', surely it's all in the journey? And if it's all in the journey, it is imperative that we have fun whilst we're on it.

I don't believe I have ever met anyone who is passionate about a job they hate. It becomes extremely hard to do your best in that place of distress.

It is therefore my surmise that the seed sown in you at some point in your life, that is part of your purpose, will be something you want to be passionate about. This then puts you in a place where you want without hesitation to do the best you can.

Perhaps you already know what your purpose is and it is one that you are passionate about. If not however, it's time to get excited and expectant. When you know your purpose procrastination stops being an issue and motivation develops a new meaning.

As a young child I was not very good at anything, or that's certainly how it felt. I wasn't academic, didn't like reading, and was more content climbing trees. Later, I never went through the phase that other girls did of learning the art of applying make-up and I was certainly never fashion-conscious. I wasn't talented and couldn't see a defined path ahead for me to take. What possible purpose did I have?

I grew up knowing many disabled children, as my mother had set up the Abingdon Riding for the Disabled Group when I was eight.

During my time living in the Kalahari Desert, I had a dream, which I believe was instigated by my faith and a Swiss couple on safari who talked in detail about their house in the mountains. I myself had only been to the mountains once, in 1986 with my sister Sarah, and I had been awestruck by its beauty then.

My dream brought together disabled children and the mountains, and was filled with laughter and achievement, support, thrills, confidence, growth and mindset shifts. I know that's what it was about because I woke knowing that the children in my dream, who hadn't before, were now starting to believe in themselves. This dream was the beginning of what was to become a major part of my life. An awesome privilege. A complete and utter joy.

Being part of the SADA trips saw me come more alive than ever before. I can relate well to the description of the boiler. If it is working, a pilot light comes on. Often people tick along with that pilot light on but without passion, lacking that sense of purpose to their day. When you find that 'thing' and the passion rises in you, it's like the boom of the boiler as it kicks in. That's exactly what I felt when I was part of the team running SADA. I also later felt that 'boom' when going voluntarily into prisons.

I discovered that a large part of my purpose was to build people up and help them see how precious they are, irrespective of their situation or ability in that moment, and I am passionate about doing that.

When you close your eyes and imagine sunrise on the rock of the Grand Canyon or freshly fallen snow covering a sleepy city, how long can you hold that thought? Does it sink in or is it merely a picture that comes and goes, slicing the top of your subconscious mind only to be taken over by the dread of today, as the knot inside reminds you of the situation you are still in?

Are you trapped in a life that seems to have ambushed you? Do you daydream of a different life? Of someone else's life? Or maybe you're feeling like there's something missing.

Make a Change

Don't be that person stuck in the shadow of relentless sameness: unfulfilled, controlled, and frustrated. Start exploring possibilities. Try new things. Talk to new people about what they love. Read, learn, and dive head-first into what moves you.

If your life is unsatisfied, even draining you, and only scraps of happiness are to be found, I guarantee you are not doing what you love, it's time to make a change.

I have been around a lot of people who complicate their circumstances and if you are like that I suggest you look at simplifying life as much as you can. When something's not working, quit it fast. More often than not people stay in situations, relationships, and jobs that they are unhappy in and possibly hate and find themselves shrivelling up inside.

If you are waiting until you know exactly what you are going to do next, trying to work everything out first, you may find that keeps you where you are. When caught in the never-ending busy-ness of everyday life, the idea of finding even more time and energy to lift yourself out of your current situation can be exhausting and overwhelming.

But it is a choice to conquer fear and step away from what is stealing your energy, time, and your life.

If you were to write down a summary of the year ahead as though it had happened and as if it were the best year ever, as mentioned in the chapter before, what would you write? If you were to paint it, how would it look? When you think about it, is there is something specific that makes you smile a lot, and then whatever it is, is a good place to start.

You can create something from scratch – just the way you want it – from your own passionate imaginings.

I hope you understand the importance of feeling passion in what you do. Please don't underestimate how it changes your day, your world, your life. Just imagine being excited and glad to wake each morning; to have the desire to be the best you can be every day and to draw people to you by your energy and enthusiasm. These characteristics alone are enormously attractive to others, because they too are desperate for them.

Out of Africa

After I returned from Africa, I went to over 30 interviews before deciding that the time had come to accept the next job I was offered. Oh boy! It was selling products to the pharmaceutical industry in a 'dog eat dog' environment where sharks tried to eat you for breakfast and people were prepared to do absolutely anything to meet sales targets. I would have taken it, but then another far more suitable job came up.

This job, however, was still not the one for me but I had no idea what I was good at at that time. I felt like I was treading water waiting to find out what I should and could do. I was grabbing at anything that came my way because I was allowing the pressures of those things outside of me to dictate and direct where I went. In doing that, it seemed money came before happiness. I was made aware regularly of how short life was and didn't want regrets or 'what ifs'. It took a couple of years before I took a really good look at who I was and what up until then had given me the greatest joy.

In speaking to colleagues recently, several said they had come to understand that their lack of happiness was rooted in their lack of passion. Finding passion is like finding your own road map.

To help find it you need to slow down. You need to change what you say about yourself and learn what makes you unique. Uniqueness is a beautiful thing and is something that will never change. Focus on things that you like and use affirmations every day. See if you can recognise recurring themes in your life, as these create a pattern which you need to follow or change. Perhaps you are drawn to something again and again but in not slowing down and taking time to think, you have failed to notice an obvious direction that's staring you in the face.

I suggest you write down a little of what you think and feel each day. It can be an eye-opener when you read the week back to yourself. Always focus on fun, what you love to do and what makes you smile. Push past fear. Maybe in doing this you have an idea that excites you and then a voice in your head says, 'I will do it when… we have more money, or when I have more experience or more time…' If those words become reality, I am afraid the idea you were thinking about will never happen. Those words are merely a mask of fear. Fear will not only stop you making progress, it may stop you from finding your purpose and your passion at all.

It's good to follow your curiosity and uncover your less obvious interests. Those interests tap into the unique motivation that separates you from others. Going after them sets you on a path of unlocking more of who you are and your creativity.

If you are wanting to spend your life doing something you love, the best way to start is to make financial concerns secondary. If you don't, and the amount of money you earn is your primary criteria and goal, you will instantly limit your options and may get nowhere in tapping into what you love. On the other hand, if you allow yourself to pursue your curiosity, you will find yourself in the position of power where purpose and passion is found and then be in a place to earn money on your terms.

I mentioned earlier how you can draw people to yourself by your attitude and enthusiasm. Think about who you are drawn to and inspired by, and why. Who pushes you to places you couldn't get to on your own? It's time to start spending more time around them. What exactly are you drawn to in them? Is it their attitude, their attributes and qualities or perhaps what they do? Are they living your dream?

Chasing the Dragon

When I was eighteen years old I was given a book called 'Chasing the Dragon' by a woman called Jackie Pullinger who worked in the back streets of Hong Kong.

Jackie had always wanted to become a missionary and after studying music at university had applied to numerous organisations. She was turned down by them all because of her age and lack of experience. In 1966, aged 22, she gathered up all her money and bought a passage on the cheapest boat she could find to Hong Kong. She only had enough for a one-way ticket, so there was no turning back. She was determined to do what she knew her purpose was and has been passionate in helping thousands, including people from the most dangerous triad gangs, to turn their lives around.

Jackie had such passion that her determination and perseverance got her to where she wanted to be and where she felt she should be. With this passion came her desire to do the very best she could every day. This showed over the weeks, months, and years in the number of lives touched and changed, healed and restored. The changes that came about in the darkest parts of the old walled city are still happening today because one young lady set out to fulfil her purpose.

I was so drawn by her bullish determination. The way in which, at such a young age, she stood tall and pushed through every barrier of negativity and fear, and it was such a breath of fresh air and made me want to be like her. I was so excited to believe, grasp, and take hold of the fact that 'You can be what you want', 'You are what you say' and at the end of the day 'You are answerable to you and only you.'

Don't let someone else be the ruler of your destiny. I have no doubt that it was her influence that was part of the reason I flew out to Africa to work in the bush at the age of 21.

To Boldy Go

I have been fortunate enough to spend time with people who shed light on a path I could not have walked alone. They are people I have wanted to learn from, people I have wanted to mimic and be like, people I have looked up to, who I have respected and admired.

When Roger Bannister staggered everyone by running the first four-minute mile in my home city of Oxford, it was not long before others too achieved it. He set the mark and proved it do-able, and that created shifts in other people's thinking as to what really was achievable by them. He was highly admired and runners aspired to be like him. Although many have broken that record since, Roger Bannister will always be remembered. His positive, determined attitude got him there first, and everyone else merely followed.

When you spend your time around people and listen to them, it will have an effect on your journey. If they are positive people who do you good, they will help you go to those places you've never dared go before and, as if blindfolded, encourage you to take that step of faith where the mask of fear has denied you entry. They will set you free to discover that seed that I promise has been planted in you. Your gifts will then unfold, your boiler will boom and you will find a new dimension to life.

Winston Churchill once said, 'Success is not final, failure is not fatal: it is the courage to continue that counts.'

I want you to uncover a plethora of little pearls of wisdom along your journey's path as you discover your passion and live your purpose, coming from that place of inner contentment.

Look at passion as if it were a living, breathing thing. If you feed it, it will grow and thrive and expand, filling your life with joy and happiness. If you don't, it will eventually do what all living things do when they are not fed: die.

When you do this and you start loving what you do, you can choose what degree of passion you put into it. The wonderful thing is, it is likely to inspire you to be passionate about a lot more of your life. My amazing three boys, Ben, Josh, and Jacob, have listened to me say on numerous occasions, 'If you do that with passion, it'll be a lot more fun, and a lot less painful.' You can choose to get up tomorrow morning and be passionate about everything you do. I can imagine you may be raising an eyebrow, but I challenge you to try it and see how you feel at the end of the day.

From the age of seven, my mum had said I would do something in property, as I loved to look in estate agent windows. Although I loved properties it wasn't just the buildings I was interested in but the lives and stories of people centuries earlier who had lived in them. I knew subconsciously, early on in life, that this was a part of what I would do. It was a seed, a passion, and one only fully germinated in the last few years.

It has taken me on the most extraordinary journey of discovering skills I never knew I had, stretching myself – and that's an understatement – in other areas I am now passionate about, learning and absorbing it all because I love it so much, and helping others all at the same time. I have learnt that my purpose was greater than the limitations of my environment or the challenges of my circumstances.

But at certain junctions and corners this took courage. At times I had to build brick walls to protect myself from the barrage of negativity towards me and push on regardless in order to be allowed to be me.

Remember this is about you. This is for you. Your life is no one else's and you have a unique purpose that at times others may not like.

A friend of mine in the world of property shared with me how she had been taught in life that if you want something, it's up to you to go and get it. She was determined whilst young to work out her passion and spent several years doing different degree courses, none of which hit 'that spot'.

Eventually, after taking time to look at herself and what truly interested her, she stepped into the world of art. Before, she had steered away from it, thinking that it wouldn't be a good career and that the people who mattered to her would be disappointed. But now, by putting her passion first rather than money, she is not only phenomenally happy but she has also made significant amounts of money in her spare time building up a large property portfolio.

It is a beautiful world out there, but one that goes unnoticed by many because their lives are filled with anxiety and sadness, monotony and boredom, control and not being understood, feeling trapped and fighting to see what it's all about.

I understand that, often, you need to find peace before you can really take time to notice the gift of the place in which you live. There is so much out there that is breath-taking, colours that have not been noticed and experiences waiting to unfold.

When you start from a place of contentment and live out your purpose with passion, you will find there is time to do so much more. Discovery of your true self and all that's around you gives you opportunity that you may never have known before and fulfilment from doing what is inside you cries, 'This is what life is about – this is my life and I am thankful.'

Chapter 5 : Magic Wands Don't Exist

Life is for the taking; freedom is a choice.

If you really want to do something, you'll find a way. If you don't, you'll find an excuse.

Your decision to progress and not procrastinate is yours and yours alone. Love is everything, attitude is essential, but action is paramount. Magic wands don't exist, and the life you choose won't drop into your lap without an investment of time, effort, and energy into making it happen.

No one else will do it for you. If you want to live a life of purpose, fulfilment, and passion, it's up to you to make it happen. It's time for you to turn your dreams into reality, to live life your way and to accept nothing less. I have talked about your inner core the 'bud' and the power your life will have if your core comes before everything and anything exterior to it. I have talked about how you get back to your inner self by illuminating lies, stripping them away so that the muddy waters that life can so easily stir up become glisteningly clear, and the true reflection of who you are returns. But these are just words until *you* decide to make it happen.

Opportunity means nothing until you take it. I heard someone say the other day, "Opportunity is like a six-slice apple pie with twelve guests at the table. If you sit back and wait for it to come to you, the chance is you will miss dessert."

Sometimes you have to search opportunities out and other times they land on your lap. But in either case, if you let fear or lethargy sneak in, it will steal like a thief in the night. Much of our lives are defined by opportunities – even the ones we miss.

In January 1987, when I was 21 years old, my parents and three sisters Jane, Carrie, Sarah, and I went to Kenya. For one of the weeks we were out there my sisters and I went on an overland trip in an army truck to Turkana. There on the edge of the bowl of Lake Rudolf – otherwise known as Lake Turkana – we saw something of the life of our grandfather, who had been District Officer there in 1926. It was on this trip that I was offered the opportunity to fly out to the Kalahari to drive service vehicles across the desert and cook on safaris.

"Wow," was all I could say, and excitement bubbled furiously as the 'boom' of my boiler meant I nearly took off. However, when we returned to the UK, with just three weeks before I was due to turn around and go back, the bubbles simmered, reality kicked in, and fear, lies about inadequacy and incompetence rose up to greet me and I was a breath away from turning down the opportunity.

Taking Action

The trouble is, opportunities are often missed because people are living in a state of victimisation and as a victim with a no-escape attitude. If this causes alarm bells to ring with you, understand that being a victim is never because those opportunities weren't or aren't available to you, but because you've chosen to live a victim's life. You have been created to prosper in your work and be a blessing. Your view of yourself – your core – may be part of where your situation and hardships stem from.

So... you see action is required. Belief in yourself and determination are musts, and both perseverance and diligence are ingredients that you need to commit to.

It is so true that whatever you choose to fill your journey with will come to define who you are. So if you aren't already, now is the time to start filling your journey with amazing things, experiences, and people. Coming from that place of contentment, your expanding formation will be one that pleases you, just like a potter gently moulding an exquisite pot from a lump of clay.

Doing is living. Too many people let life slip by because it's easier not to do than to do. Fulfilment doesn't enter their vocabulary because it's more of a mythical word that they have no concept could become reality.

Angelina Jolie said, "If you ask people what they've always wanted to do, most people haven't done it - and that breaks my heart."

What if life didn't happen *to* you, it happened *for* you? What if I examined all of the crap that had happened to me before and saw where it led me? What if I realised there was a purpose for every circumstance of difficulty, struggle, pain, and trauma? How would my perspective change if I realised that my quality of life is directly related to my reactions?

Would I stop and appreciate those moments of darkness if I realised that they are necessary to guide me to the light in my life? With a change in focus, you can change your life. If this is what you want, realise that you have the power to do it. Instead of waiting for life to happen, make it happen. Instead for waiting for a change, create a change.

Passion Requires Action

You *can* start living a life of deep passion, doing what you love, and loving what you do. The question is: 'Are you going to?' because – it's all in the action. Passion can only come out of doing.

People often react terribly to being called lazy. Their defence barriers go up as if they have been caught in the headlights. The thing is that laziness isn't only unproductive but it also creates whole heaps of dissatisfaction within people's lives. It is a decision to be like this, to adopt an attitude that doesn't give room for passion or progress.

There is a scene in the film *The Karate Kid* where the boy goes to his teacher's yard and drops his coat on the floor. In previous scenes he drops his coat on the floor whenever he enters his home, never bothering to hang it up. His teacher calls him over and tells him to pick the coat up and put it on the hook. He then tells him to take it off the hook and put it on the floor. He asks him again to pick it up and put it on the hook and then to take it off and put it on the floor. He continues this for a long time – not for minutes but for hours.

As it happens, in the film, the teacher is not simply teaching the boy that laziness, attitude, and respect count for so much, but is also, without the boy's knowledge, teaching him a move to better his karate skills.

I am sure he thought twice before he ever dropped his coat on the floor again.

Making It Happen

Framed in my house are the words, 'Some people want it to happen, some wish it would happen, others make it happen'.

There is no longer time or space for being a victim, for bad attitude, laziness, or for being envious of others' successes. There is no longer reason to point the finger; you will see that when you do, there are three pointing back at you. These actions and attitudes will just give unfounded reason to take little or no action. It is time to choose between the camps that divide our population – those that wish but stay parked up, and those who know what they want and hit the ground running.

I speak to many people and so often they get stuck in taking that step of change because fear of the unknown rears its ugly head. I don't even need to hear them say, "I have to be sure" – their worried facial expressions say it all. They want everything laid out, numbered and measured, on a grid: a plan that they can study, pinned on a board, so they can see it all and just follow it.

I have a good friend who is so talented, so gifted; she has an aura about her but she doesn't see it or believe it. Through nothing other than fear and lack of self-belief she is living life in neutral. She copes daily in a job she hates but pretends is OK just so she doesn't have to take that step of faith, and risk letting herself and everyone she loves down. The saddest thing is that her undiscovered passions will be a source of happiness that is never realised.

Nelson Mandela said, "There is no passion to be found playing small – in settling for a life that is less than the one you are capable of living."

You'll never know what gets you up and out of bed in the morning until you explore your possibilities and discover the seed planted in you. Thinking too long about doing something is often the reason it never gets done and in order to be creative we must lose our fear of being wrong.

There is no scarcity of opportunity to make a living at what you love; there's only scarcity in deciding to make it happen. Instead, be one of the minority and make it happen for you.

I've done software sales and voluntary work with disabled children and prisoners. I have worked as an agent for overseas properties and done both mentoring and coaching. I have looked after a yard full of horses and written articles for local newspapers. I have written one book and am in the process of writing another. I have produced a children's dinner party game and am a property investor. I have travelled extensively and have loved my life and the colours in it. Much of the time when I was doing these things money was tight and I scraped my way through situations and positions that I wasn't really qualified to be in. Some I have liked, enjoying the stretch and learning that growth begins at the end of my comfort zone. Others I have loved. But it was by looking back and taking note of the times I was at my happiest that I worked out my passion.

It is so true that often, we live life forwards but we understand it backwards. But if you want to fly, you have to give up the things that weigh you down.

It's about rising to the challenge, taking hold of what's on offer and transforming your life by sorting inside, so that the plan outside unfurls and you can start living in a way that's right for you.

But don't wait until the conditions are perfect to begin because it's beginning that makes the conditions perfect. The world is your oyster if you have an attitude that allows you to conquer, make the truth matter, and no longer be a victim but victorious.

The fact that you may be struggling does not mean you are failing and it is true that every great success requires some kind of struggle to get there. Don't carry your mistakes around with you, instead place them under your feet and use them as stepping stones to learn from and progress. You are a glorious work in progress. There is no need for perfectionism, just the desire to be the best you can be as yourself in the moment.

A Change In Attitude

It is also true, however, that some are waiting or hoping for things to happen but they are working on the wrong things.

I recently listened to the very sad story of a lady who had a very tough childhood full of rejection. She realised at the age of five that she would never be anything more than the unwanted child. She wasn't the adored first child but the second of two girls in a family in China where it was deemed a disgrace not to have a boy. The third child was not only the doted-on youngest, but also the boy that was required.

There was much more to the story but it left her seriously wounded, with absolutely no self-worth or value. She moved to England and became very successful and achieved much, but remained unhappy and had times of serious depression. She had aspirations to help less fortunate families but even in her quest to do that she found no fulfilment, just emptiness, and a deep sense of loneliness and 'aloneness'.

I asked her the question, "On a scale of 1-10 what do you think of yourself?" and she replied, "Minus 20."

I said, "My friend that is where you need to begin."

At her core was nothing – she felt meaningless, unimportant, and forgotten. She was hiding from the pain of the past but accepting the lies that were in it. In her situation, it wasn't a case of being lazy or believing that she could or couldn't achieve: she was doing in order to forget, and achieving to prove her worth. She was allowing the lies of the past and the petals of the present – those things exterior to her – to make her who she was. This resulted in a mortified, tired, confused, and unhappy person.

Action needs to be taken but from the inside out, never the outside in.

Reinhold Niebuhr sums this up beautifully, 'God grant me the serenity to accept the things I cannot change, courage to change the things I can, and wisdom to know the difference.'

Your dreams, your aspirations, your goals and your hope are there for the taking. So know truth, take those steps forward and see how a change in attitude and action creates change in your world.

Chapter 6 : You Need to Stop Comparing

In our society there is so much pressure, competitiveness, envy, and lack of satisfaction.

This is destructive, and drives us away from our unique purpose. It distorts our vision and ruins any passion we may have discovered as we focus on others and compare ourselves enviously with them.

Focusing on someone else will only cause you to regret who you aren't.

Life isn't graded on a curve. How you measure up against others has absolutely no importance in your life.

Teddy Roosevelt said, "Comparison is the thief of joy."

This has to be my most-used quote, because it holds so much truth. Negative comparison steals from you, it drains you of energy, and destroys.

Some comparison can result in admiration, inspiration, and motivation. It can make us grateful that we can look at others and desire more for ourselves. It can make us humble and realise that we still have a long way to go. But in this chapter I am addressing the comparison that steals your joy, your relationships, your motivation, and so much more. Comparison that paralyses, leaves you confused, fearful of the future, and insecure about who you truly are.

I met two young lads on a course once. They were great friends. One was very academic, good looking and sporty but had no self-worth. The other was not academic at all but within his core he had enormous self-belief. The more academic of the two struggled to find friendships but the non-academic one with self-worth drew people to him. The first of the two seemed to have everything going for him, yet he yearned to have the confidence of the other, to the point that he thought that if he did the same activities, life would come right.

His friend had many difficult times academically but was content within himself. His confidence, untainted by arrogance, had allowed him to find his passion with ease. He wasn't influenced by negative undertones or anything that threw him off course. He was on a mission to live life with passion and to make sure, even with some fairly high hurdles, that he did what he was born to do. Both had a purpose: they were completely different from each other and would never be the same. So why did one compare with the other?

If you want to be the best that you can be, make a decision to stop comparing as its destructive ways could possibly even end your dream before it starts. Be good to yourself; focus on all that is you. The more centred you are, the easier this is. You have been made precious. 'You are enough' and you need to understand on a deep level that there is no place for inferiority. The only time someone else can make you feel inferior is with your consent. You have unique attributes and abilities, thoughts, ideas and goals, and your own way of interpreting ambition, success, freedom, faith, and love.

Do you compare who you are – your life, your home, your children, your partner, your business success, your clothes, your holidays, your monetary worth, or anything else with other people's? This question may reveal some surprises. If it does, don't run from them but embrace them. Think about how these comparisons make you feel. They are likely to create negative thoughts that sap your energy and throw filth in the face of all that has worth. They distort the truth and stunt your growth, but most of all they steal your joy.

I met a lady some years ago who was already a very successful business woman when she decided to get into property. She had set herself a goal to acquire two properties within a twelve-week time frame. She was a doer, an achiever, and was determined and driven.

Chasing Success

She hit her goal, which was no mean task and for a brief moment she had a wry smile, as if pleased with her results. Then sadly, within moments, she was comparing her results against those of someone else and that moment of joy was gone. Her success meant nothing and I watched her chasing more and more, never knowing satisfaction or contentment, trying to better those around her and reprimanding herself if she fell short. Today she hasn't changed.

How does that give opportunity for deep joy, big smiles, passion, excitement, warmth, and gratitude? It doesn't: it's stolen!

It was all about having more than X or being better than Y – and to what end? In this place enjoyment is elusive, peace is a far-fetched myth, reaching your goal is never enough, and, instead of resting, you become restless.

Comparison doesn't just leave you feeling insecure and unworthy, it lets fear, shame, anxiety, and inferiority have a massive party in your heart and mind. It becomes a weapon that is capable of destroying who you are.

You are you, not anyone else. Their life is not your life and your life is not theirs. You may have focused on their results but you don't know what they went through to get them. They will have their own issues – ones that you don't have. It's OK to let them be their best too, because blowing out their candle doesn't make yours shine any brighter. Instead of comparing and distorting the journey that you are on by focusing on the wrong person, be focused on you and be happy for them.

Annie is a very good friend of mine with a beautiful singing voice, and she has sung in a band for a few years. She told me recently with great excitement that they had been asked to be the support band for Charlie Dore, who is famous in the folk singing world. Memories flooded Annie of dancing on summer nights to 'Pilot of the Airwaves'. Just days before the gig, Charlie contacted Annie and asked if she and another member of the band would be prepared to do some numbers with her. Of course, albeit wracked with nerves, she said they would. They had the most amazing night which was capped off by an audience member asking Annie for her autograph. As she told me this, excitement welled up in me, and I was so happy and so proud of her. I think the joy I felt equalled hers and all I wanted to do was celebrate.

Let your response to the successes of others be one that lifts them.

Don't pop their bubble or shatter their moment. When you respond positively you add significantly to your life and the sun shines in your soul, just as responding negatively with thoughts of comparison and envy takes significantly from your life and makes the black clouds gather, weighing in your soul and causing dullness and dissatisfaction. You will find at this point that you need to let things go, simply for the reason that they are heavy.

The opposite of comparing with others is learning from them and celebrating with them. It doesn't matter whether what they have achieved or experienced relates in any way to what you are doing or the results you are pursuing.

The Key to Success

Some journeys made years ago across miles of land now only take a few hours by car, but those who used to walk took days. This gave them time to think, to look up at the sky and around at the hills and fields. It gave them time with people. We've lost a lot of that in the mad rush we call modern life. We move so fast that we have to keep our eyes on the road, with no time for the landscape or the people in it. If you do stop you are probably told to move on for blocking the way.

Relationships are key to your success. Relationships with yourself, and all the people in your world will determine whether you are living a sustainable lifestyle but with little to no contentment, living in the back streets where all hope is lost, or living as a king or queen. Which are you?

Bad relationships will cause bitterness, anger, envy, and pain. Good relationships will create growth, trust, integrity, and joy. Don't let your life be dragged into the gutter where in your innermost self you are running from nothingness, where your feet are soft and your heart is hard.

You weren't given your life to waste it believing you are nothing – incapable, less than others, and insignificant. You are spectacular. Don't let the giant of comparison dictate any of your moves. As you look over your shoulder, constantly comparing to others' situations, results, aspirations, and goals, you will be knocked off track. You may not realise it, but by doing this you are self-destructing. Maybe only a little at a time, but by comparing with others you are denying yourself joy, and fulfilment, and forgetting that you are the only you that there will ever be. So be grateful for who you are and get up, get out, and be determined to be your best.

It's time to concentrate on the person you've been made to be, your goal, and your passion and in doing so you will find the power to perform. This comes from deep within when you focus on your purpose and leave other people's purposes to them. It allows you to enjoy your journey, your little steps forward that may be small but are instrumental. Understand that your purpose is in your journey; faith en-route makes everything surmountable and the destination is merely where you end up, whether that's with money, a family, a good business, a charity, knowledge, or growth.

Stepping Stones

When I was in the process of buying the chalet, I saw it like two riverbanks with stepping-stones between them. When we were growing up we used to go camping in the Dordogne. In part of the river there were stepping-stones to walk across. Some were fairly precarious and it was a challenge to see how far we could get.

Whilst attempting to purchase the chalet I experienced all number of emotions as I trod stones that changed my thinking, stretched my understanding, challenged my doubting, and grew me immensely. I never expected to get to the other side, but I also never expected not to get there. The point was, the destination was not what mattered, but the journey.

Imagine for a moment getting to the other side without any growth, difficulties, stretches, learning, experiences, or lifelong memories – just landing there. How does that feel? Or perhaps having the journey of a lifetime, meeting people who change your course, learning a bit more from each step about the person you are, knowing encouragement and celebration but not getting to the bank that you originally set out to reach. Which would you prefer?

The stones that I trod were sometimes pointed and hard to balance on. That was when I thought the journey was coming to an end, but instead the doors just opened. There were then other, very flat stones, from which my pride and elements of arrogance would almost cause me to drown.

Yes, I got to the other side and from there began a different journey of blessings, but I learnt that it was the experience en route – the passage of pain, frustration, joy, exhilaration, and hopeful expectation – that counted.

Don't let the joy be stolen from your journeys by comparing them with others'; they are yours to be trodden. But it's your choice, either to move on and grab hold of what's on offer to you in being who you are, or to become a prisoner to all that comparison brings.

You know what else steals joy on your journey? Perfectionism. So often our need to be perfect makes us envy, as we compare with those who have what we don't.

When you look at what other people have and you feel a tug, step back and ask the question why? Even if it's just a small tug. So often it's coupled with the need for perfectionism, or to be the blue-eyed boy, or to feel more valued and important than the next person. All this does is give room for you to tear yourself to pieces with the destructiveness of criticism and daily guilt and agonising over every detail of failure when you underachieve compared to someone else.

Can you see how negative that is? Even if this only applies slightly to you, each time it happens, it chips away at you and your destination changes through default because of your attitude and responses.

When you go out of your way to be better than someone else, or knock yourself inwardly when you discover their results are better, what exactly are you saying to yourself? Perhaps being equal to, or better than someone else allows for accolades which make you feel worthy and help to create wholeness.

The truth is, wholeness lies in looking at yourself, with all your faults, and accepting what you see, in love. Then you can spend your energies not striving for perfectionism and being better than others but developing your relationships *with* each other.

Home Run

I once watched a film with a scene that has had a lasting impact on me.

A young lad was needing to hit a 59er in baseball to win a crucial match. He had only ever hit a 39er and was lacking confidence. He was doubting his ability and assuming the result. His coach went up to him and asked, "Do you believe God can do this through you?" When the lad said, "Yes", the coach said, "Well you do your best, and let him do the rest."

Now you may think that is crazy, but even if you're not so sure about what God can or can't do, can you tell me why your best is not enough?

When you focus on your heart, mind, and soul, when you keep looking in and giving out, serving with humility, you will find that it's not the results that help you find your way to contentment, but the process. When you do this there will no longer be the urge to compare. You will find that having set your goals according to what you desire, how other people do no longer matters. Any potential arrogance that cocoons you and restricts your growth is shed. Jealousy no longer pushes things away as gratitude makes room for new things to come.

Absorb the truth that there is no need to struggle, to compare and be compared, to earn your right at the front of the queue. Just hold on to the certainty that *you are about you* and you can make that fantastically exciting or not. The choice is yours.

Be someone who understands your limitations without feeling anger towards those who don't have them. Someone who can look at excellence and feel admiration, not indignation. Feel free to observe reality as it is without allowing it to steal your joy, and train your heart for greater things, so that you can support others and be supported by them on your journey.

Letting Go

I recall vividly standing in my mum and dad's garden at the age of 18. A couple had come over with their flock of children and everyone was chatting as the hoards ran riot around us. Mary and Jim had been married for several years and there was an unmistakable note of animosity and antagonism when she opened her mouth. He was a placid man trying to please. I remember her speaking on and off the whole time about the need for him to do more overtime, to work harder and produce more money. It wasn't an unpleasant time but that conversation had a profound effect on me.

As Mary made demands and spoke of her need for money to acquire, buy, and get hold of the materialistic things her friends had, it became more and more apparent that it was all about keeping up with the Joneses – wanting more of, or equal to, or better than. What saddened me was the pressure, the desperation in her to have, and the control that went with it.

I remember making a decision in my subconscious mind that I would never be like that to the person I married, but the opposite. I wanted to help alleviate pressure, not create it. I believed it wouldn't be hard for me because of my faith. I knew that money and material things didn't and wouldn't come first but I was also aware that the pressures of the world would still be ready to pounce in situations I had yet to experience, understand, or consider. I didn't yet know the man I would marry and, based on that mild conversation that my head and heart had recorded, I had the desire to step out and create. I still believe today that as well as the dream I had in Africa, the day in the garden was another catalyst in my determination to achieve young despite having none of the normal requirements.

It is often good to get lost in something greater than we are, such as walking across the knife-edge bridge under Victoria Falls with a full circle of rainbow around you from the spray, or being at the top of the highest mountain and looking down over all the others, and realising that you are tiny. The decision to be humble before greater things can help you look beyond your insufficiencies, and what little more someone has than you do. What do your petty score sheets look like in the face of beauty and greatness?

To be truly wealthy is not to have all things but to be content with what you have. There has never been another person like you since time began, so there is nothing and no earthly being to compare or compete with. Stand tall, be bold, be excited, and take steps of faith as you begin your journey. Jump into that purpose destined for you, and start building on those solid foundations of contentment, which will create exponential growth in all areas of your life.

Chapter 7 : Moving from Struggle to Grace

What is your struggle today?

Is it life as a whole, or specific compartments of your life? When you are in that place of struggle, your insides knotted and turmoil bubbling like a volcano spitting out lava, it can be so hard to believe that peace is a genuine state of heart and mind available to you.

An amazing variety of seemingly incompatible people and activities can co-exist in your life with harmony and a sense of order when you have peace and assurance in the core of yourself. With a strength that comes from that healthy centre of self-worth and love, it is so much easier and more natural to be vulnerable without shame and to be able to accept your emotions without judgement as you realise that you are more than your emotions, thoughts, fears, and personality.

Emotions are fickle; they come and go and they need to no longer dictate your way forward. Your thoughts are yours to control and courage defies fear. The more you realise these truths, the easier it becomes for you to move from struggle into the arms of grace.

Like so many of us, I have had struggles to get through and, more recently, some that have seemed enormous. In that time I have seen the power of inner contentment help me ride the storm and come out the other side.

Close your eyes and imagine a boat in a fierce storm. Huge waves are breaking against the boat which, although a reasonable size, is tiny against the vastness of the ocean. It's frightening and can take its toll. But it dies down and then you learn from it, and your skills increase. You are able to cope with those storms when they arise and enjoy your journey on peaceful waters at other times.

So often, however, this is not the case. When the tectonic plates move in the depths of the sea they have an adverse effect on all that is above. This creates tsunamis, which cause devastation. It all starts from below, from within, and causes havoc above.

If you are churning, rumbling, and knotted inside, you have the beginnings of a tsunami in you, which could be catastrophic on the surface, or it could just continue to rumble causing a continual niggling unrest and stress.

The boat in the storm represents what life can throw at us. In that scenario, the seas below are completely calm and actually the deeper you go, the more peaceful it gets. The life down there is extraordinarily beautiful, unseen, unscathed, untouched by the storms above.

Ride the Waves

It's time to make your 'below the surface' – the deeper you – peaceful. When you run into storms, you will ride and come out the other side wiser and more whole, without regret.

You have to see first, however, that it *is* possible to move from tirelessly striving to having endless favour and blessing. Believing in yourself and being excited about who you have been made to be will be part of the inner peace, which in itself will help to do away with the striving and struggle.

I believe that this then allows you to live as you were meant to or as you would choose. If you find yourself wandering in the rubble of yesterday's hope, weighed down with burdens and barely standing, something has to change. If it doesn't, life will be an enormous effort just waiting to end.

Perhaps you are struggling for approval, or to make someone proud or pleased with you. It is so easy in this place to strive and struggle to be someone you're not – or perhaps to be the person you were made to be but find yourself a little more broken each day, and never enough for the one you so desperately want to please. The struggle in this situation can go on for years, and what you don't realise is that whilst it is happening, for every moment you don't succeed in pleasing that person, they are chipping away a little more at the person you are.

It is time to stand upright and stop looking for approval and support from those who are never going to give it. It's time to stop letting them knock you again and again with condemnation and lies. Where love is concerned, I know it is hard but if you continue to struggle in trying to please someone who will never be pleased, you will find it tearing at your soul, shattering your confidence, and potentially sending you seeking approval in the wrong places.

We all want peace. Inner peace is more precious than gold. Life changes phenomenally when peace reigns and chaos, struggle, and confusion are gone. This doesn't mean life is easy or that there won't be storms on the surface, but it's the deep peace and contentment within that continually reminds us of the gift that life is and the privilege we have in living it. Feelings and emotions come and go, but where peace is found, your still, conscious self stays the same.

Whether your struggle is financial, emotional, physical, or spiritual, you will need to let go of it. You can get so used to struggling that it becomes your security, something you hide behind so as not to have to move on – something that has become part of who you are. If this is the case, you have allowed the things outside you to dictate who you have become. You can only lose what you cling to, and you need courage here to let go of what's become necessary and familiar.

There is a call to freedom in this, a confidence that banishes all that weighs you down. Timidity lessens as confidence rises and you make the choice to walk away from struggle, to let go of the past and press on towards the future.

Struggle No More

So what is your struggle? Is it one you speak of and want to resolve?

This is the storm on the surface that you have to ride. Or is it unrest and churning below, that causes a constant storm on the surface that never ceases? Or perhaps your storm is hidden, one you don't talk about? If that is the case, whatever compartment of your life you are struggling in, the first thing you need to do is stop denying it. Stop trying to avoid it by telling the world that everything is all right, that what you are doing is OK, that things could be worse. This is your one shot at life so don't accept mediocrity and stop allowing fear to dictate its quality.

Your thoughts are so powerful in everyday life. They have a profound effect on the way in which your life turns out. They come and go without permission: sometimes they surprise, shock, or overpower you. Thoughts can take you to the limit, the highest mountain, the deepest oceans and beyond into the cosmos, to distant galaxies and boundless space. Sometimes a thought takes hold of you and won't let go.

Recently I had to have a medical in order to get life cover to refinance my guest house. The tests were fine and I went to ask the doctor to rush the report through as time was of the essence. Whilst I was there he asked to have a look at a bruise that I'd got some weeks previously. He decided that he wanted to get some tests done. Unfortunately, one of the results came back abnormal, and as the tests were done before the report was written, the ambiguous results of the additional, unnecessary test had to go on the report – and my cover was turned down.

Now, bearing in mind it had taken me two years to get the refinance sorted, I could have been seriously churned up by this. It was because of grace, however, that I rode the storm and managed to do so with peace at my side.

In your struggles what thoughts stick like limpets to your mind?

Are they negative or positive, and are they helping you to be all you can be? If you haven't already, write down any repetitive thoughts you have, or, even better, keep a diary of daily thoughts. Then at the end of each week read through them and determine whether they are positive or negative, how they make you feel and whether they are significant to the struggles in your world.

It is so true that how we respond and react to a situation determines what happens next.

All struggles are different. Some seem so big that you may wish for the resulting tsunami to wipe you out with the struggle. Some are there bubbling under the surface, and some have become your life, creating a monotony filled with nothing more than coping and existence.

It's so true that as a race of people we put unbelievable pressure on ourselves: pressure to perform, produce, create – the most, the best, enough, and more. We struggle to be more than we are, or to be what we aren't. Then we get frustrated with ourselves and things come crashing down as we proclaim ourselves hopeless. We get snared in a thicket of thorns, and the more we struggle the more we tear at who we are.

Let's get back to you. Why should you move from struggle to grace? Simply to enjoy life and be blessed. Is that possible? Yes, it is, even through tough times. You have gifts that are specific to you and, dependent on your attitude and mindset, they will be part of your journey to success and fulfilment.

Where There's Hope

I was speaking in prison one day on this subject when two of the inmates caused a bit of a ruction. We were nearly at the point of pressing the green button for immediate assistance but they settled and the meeting resumed. There was much going on for both of them but it was later that I heard the story behind the stress of that day and the storm that one of them was trying to ride. The confines of the prison and the pounding of the problem was perpetual and there seemed to be no end in sight.

Some of his problem was within his control and some was not. He needed to let go of that which he could do nothing about and look at how he could positively deal with the other aspects of the problem. He was a negotiator, articulate, and good with people. It's so sad how often you have to be at your lowest ebb to be ready to hear, to listen, and be still, almost with an attitude of having nothing to lose.

On that cold October day in a freezing chapel he sat, deeply engaged in what he heard as if for the first time. The thought that he had gifts and a purpose specifically for him was remarkable to him. He was blown away by the realisation that even he had a future of hope, and that he could ride the storms he was experiencing and reach a place of calm if he dealt with his issues in a different way.

Are you caught up in things you can't control, that half the time you can't even understand? It's so easy to feel lost and swallowed up, and to believe that your effort is useless. But what are you hearing? Is it truth about yourself, your worth, your purpose, or is it not?

A group of us were climbing an overgrown hill – I think of it as a small mountain – several years ago and I was quite unfit. We were walking on a steep, narrow, rocky path and I remember being exhausted and shaky from lack of sustenance. Heart hammering and blood pumping I'd reach the top of every small achievement, look up and see the summit ahead, still painfully high. It was hard.

Life can be like that. Are you finding that without much effort you can feel hurt? I have certainly felt that each hill climbed leads to another and another and yet another.

Struggle will find you and stick to you if you allow it to. Don't invite it in or allow it to stay.

Keep Your Head Up

I read once, 'We used to look up at the sky and wonder at our place in the stars. Now we just look down and worry about our place in the dirt.'

If that is you, by your attitude and thought pattern you are inviting negativity and struggle into your day, your world. You absolutely do not belong in the dirt or anywhere that you see as being for losers or those less fortunate. Chickens peck at the ground, in the dirt, and can't fly. Lift your head out of the mud. Don't choose to be like them but be like an eagle. When you go to a window look up at the sky, not down at the dirt. When you are working and going about your day, make a conscious effort to look up, especially when things are tougher. This *will* make a difference.

I recall the terrifying day the mist came down on Beauregard, my favourite mountain in La Clusaz. I was with my twin sister Sarah and the thick sheet of white meant I couldn't see my hand in front of my face. "Keep your head up," she kept saying as the mist thinned and we could see a little more, "Keep your head up".

In many situations you will find that looking up is not only helpful but powerfully conducive to creating a healthier state of mind, a more positive attitude, a more uplifting sense of being and a greater belief that there is hope.

A Leap into the Unknown

One October in Cornwall, it was a bitterly cold day. I had been up for a walk on Lobber Point; there was no wind and the grass looked pale against the grey of the bare trees. As I came down into the harbour I saw a fisherman take his net out of the water. It exploded with energy as a mass of fish wriggled frantically. He looked at them with quiet satisfaction, then gently released them into the water, giving them their freedom.

When you are caught up in never-ending tangles of selfishness, self-pity, depression, victimisation, and hopelessness, netted like a fish and thrashing around without purpose or hope, caught up in the pressures that surround you every day, do you find each struggle weakens you a little more? Perhaps it's a net of egotism or the expectations of others that hold you prisoner.

Moving from struggle to grace is life-changing and transformational. It's not a leap into the unknown but small steps into the right direction as the pressure gradually eases.

So, my friend, what about you? Do you try hard to show a calm and cool exterior that masks a multitude of doubt? An avalanche of questions that threatens to engulf and freeze your self-belief? Questions aren't always answered but it's having the courage to believe within that doubt and fear that is crucial.

It's time to take responsibility, time to try things in a new way. It's time to consciously create and move on from the struggles that have been holding you back to a place of grace where life flows.

Whether you choose to believe that or not, grace is a state of awakening to the gifts of existence, life, and love. In this place, your mind can be liberated from mental slavery and you can enjoy happiness, a relaxed mind, and boundless energy. Grace is the antidote to spiritual dis-ease, to anxiety, to paranoia, and to depression. In a state of grace, you know your purpose and you succeed in creating a life that benefits not only you but an ever-growing circle of those around you.

You can still enjoy a great life through life's challenges. What counts is not what happens to you, but how you respond to it. Consider embracing this approach and find hope every single day. You will be confronted with challenges but where struggle is, your purpose is not. So move away from it now and allow yourself the opportunity to live life to the full, to learn again how to laugh from the depths of your being. Believe in those big dreams and walk into big blessings.

Relax as you journey down the path toward the wonder of grace and the freedom it brings.

Chapter 8 : The Power of Words

This is all about your life, your opportunity, your existence, and purpose. It is all about you.

We are complex beings. The reason that deep contentment is so key is because there are so many elements outside it with which to live through, deal with, understand, and grow. If you don't first find that contentment, it is likely that you will fall on your face and sustain not just superficial wounds but potentially deep ones.

We have all been given a voice. This can be used magnificently or not. In your life, how much do you use your voice? Where would you be without it?

What you say, both out loud and 'in loud', can grow your world exponentially. It can be the reason your dreams become reality and your blessings flow. It can be the reason you find yourself surrounded by great people with genuine hearts to help you, push you on, and support you.

Your voice is to be used, but with care. We are gentle and attentive when handling a brand new instrument, or a fragile object. Be the same with your voice. It is a privilege to have such control over something so powerful, something that can be the making or breaking of today or tomorrow.

The world is an interwoven web of words and they are phenomenally important in your life. A word out of your mouth may seem of no matter but it can accomplish nearly anything, or destroy everything. It only takes a spark to set off a forest fire. A carelessly or wrongly placed word can do that. By your words, you can ruin the world, turn harmony into chaos, throw mud on a reputation, send the whole world up in smoke and go up in smoke with it. The tongue is like a two-edged sword, one that can curse one minute and bless the next.

A spring doesn't gush fresh water one day and unclean the next, and fruit trees don't get confused daily by what fruit to produce. To know fulfilment in this world, you need to tame your tongue to speak only blessings and positivity.

Negative words travel far and fast, especially destructive criticism, judgement, and gossip. They can be the reason others shrink away to nothing. Reputations can be seriously harmed and when others hear these damaging words, they're influenced in a negative way.

Words are so powerful and yet are often used so recklessly. If your words are caustic they can resemble a person thrusting a razor-sharp sword in the air and cutting people indiscriminately. Healing words, however, are gentle, encouraging, full of appropriate praise and grace, and are spoken at just the right moment.

Loose Words

Almost every one of us knows a gracious person who is gentle, humble, and not overbearing. We are drawn to them perhaps because of their genuine calm and caring character. We can all become just as attractive to others, if we commit to speak words of encouragement, kindness, and love.

If you were to be cross-examined and tested, would it become clear that your words run loose? Or would it become apparent that you build people up? Speak positivity into lives and edify them?

Several years ago, we started having family meetings once a week. We used to end the meetings with each of us choosing another family member in the room to 'build up' for the week. I wanted to teach my boys the power of positive words, and how thoughtfulness in speech makes such a difference in relationship. By focusing on one person, it didn't mean they were to be uncaring to the others but it meant consciously making a concerted effort with that person. Thinking before opening their mouths and holding their tongues, giving time to replace any unpleasant or negative words with positive, uplifting ones.

When you judge, destructively criticise, complain, gossip, or use sarcasm, you're pushing all thought of unity away. Most people don't really understand the profound effects words have on lives.

A young lady called Carol was working as an admin assistant in a large corporate organisation, where the words spoken to her for several years made her feel worthless. She had a sad lonely life and suffered from an eating disorder. She felt totally unnoticed by everyone and had got to the point of truly believing that she wouldn't be missed if she died. By the time she concluded that the answer was to end her life, she was ready. The extraordinary thing was that that same week a new member of staff arrived.

They spoke to Carol with warmth and interest in her life. They made her smile and then laugh for the first time in years. They made a difference – a massive difference. Carol's mindset changed, her heart woke up, and she felt significant, all because of carefully spoken, kind, gentle words.

Changing Minds

You have the power to effect change in your life and others by speaking, because your words are containers of power. They have the ability to carry faith or fear, blessing or cursing, life or death. They bring someone from the slums of life and make success out of them, or destroy their happiness.

If articulated in the right way words can change someone's mind and alter someone's belief. They can encourage and build up, redeem and build bridges.

There are many people who attribute their success to positive words spoken to them earlier in life. Children who heard loving, encouraging, and positive words are likely to grow up being self-confident and successful in life. But children who heard only negative words of condemnation are likely to grow up emotionally destabilised. Their lives can only be changed if they choose to illuminate the lies and start to listen only to positive and encouraging words.

A simple choice of words can make the difference between someone accepting or denying themselves. You can have a very beautiful thing to say but say it with the wrong words and it's gone!

But how about the words said to you? Have you ever felt that there was so much noise and so many words? Voices offering suggestion after suggestion, trapping you, and ensnaring your thoughts in a mass of uncertainty. Seas of opinions, conflicting, insistent, as you drift into a chaos of confusion.

Self Talk

Who do you listen to? And should you be listening to them?

Words can be wonderful or cruel, helpful or unhelpful. Often it is obvious that you should let them go straight over your head if they are blindingly negative, or destructive in any way – perhaps coming from the mouth of someone who is riddled with bitterness. Sometimes they are persuasive and take you along the wrong path. But other times words can be cleverly disguised to tear down and it is then that often confidence and character can be decimated.

It was a hot, balmy evening, and she spoke quietly, "It hurts so much. I want him to want me to be me, so badly. I want him to be pleased with me, proud of me. In my work, nothing seems good enough. Apparently I just build up his expectations. I get excited by ideas and opportunities, it's part of who I am, and I share them with him."

The self-talk continued, "The bubble is popped, the joy is gone and he asks me to tell him what results I expect that month. I can only tell him hopeful business that might be. Irrespective of the effort, I am a let-down. For him, it's all about the money, not the experiences or the journey. And heaven forbid something should go wrong with any of what I do. He scolds me and tells me it's my problem to sort out and that he knew I would produce nothing."

"The thing is", she continued, "I am affected by it for a while and then carry on thinking it won't happen again, but it does. There is so much to be excited about, so much to be grateful for, so much opportunity to laugh, but it doesn't happen because I'm not good enough."

She explains how only now she had come to realise how the bullying words had been chipping away at the person she was for years. For most of those years her only desire had been to please enough to feel worthy and hear words of approval and love.

Even coming from a place of contentment at your core, life, people, and the many facets of all that is exterior can cause you to feel exasperated – not least of all by words. But they can also be an incredible blessing, building towers of strength in the hearts of individuals.

But our ability to express, explain, describe, tell a story, teach, encourage, and be compassionate is so easy to take for granted. Your voice is a gift. I know of a man who got hit by a car when riding his bike at the age of 19. His father took him to hospital with a suspected broken leg and within a couple of hours he had an excruciating headache. Within a short period of time he had a brain haemorrhage and lost all ability to speak.

If you are born without the ability to speak, you know no difference and adapt to your disability, but aged

19, with all brain function working, how hard must that be to deal with?

The sudden loss of the ability to speak, to say words of comfort to those you love, to shout, sing, laugh, say 'I do', 'I love you', or your child's name. Imagine for a second being told that in a certain period of time your voice would vanish. How much more would you appreciate the gift that it is, and be aware of what you say? When you communicate with words, use them with care: be wise, pause, and think before you allow anything to escape your lips.

The Impact of Words

So what about words that cut? What about words that are factual that you can't control and that you don't like?

I had been in the Kalahari Desert for a few months when Mum and Dad came out to visit me. The plan was to drive into the Okavango Delta, the jewel of the Kalahari, and then on to Savuti, also known as Chobe, the heart of the Kalahari. From there we would be going to Serendela and crossing the border into Zimbabwe. I was so looking forward to walking with them over the border to Zambia and onto the knife-edge bridge under the spray of Victoria Falls.

It was nearing their arrival and Adam, my boss, announced that I had done one too many trips on my visa and wouldn't be able to join them on the second leg of the safari into Zimbabwe. *Nothing* could be done. I was gutted, devastated. I'd not seen them for so long and they were flying 2,000 miles to be with me and for half the time, due to ignorance on my part, I would not be with them. The words 'visa expired' repeated over and over in my head. I had to accept what I couldn't change and move on, although I have to admit that I couldn't for the first 24 hours. But if we don't, we use up endless amounts of energy and are cruel to ourselves.

How you respond to things you hear that you don't like is key to your growth, as it's a maturity of attitude that helps you hold your tongue and say nothing. Sometimes less is more. Silence is OK, pauses are powerful, and speaking thoughtfully and slowly is calming.

How do words make you feel? It is important to be honest with yourself. There is no space for being tough and pretending that words don't affect you. You may hit certain goals with a hard heart attitude and a loud, insensitive, or bitter voice, but the question is, will there be happiness and contentment when you reach them, or just a ticked box? Once you have noted how words make you feel, start giving out what you would like to receive. Hopefully that will mean all intimidation, bullying, and unpleasantness in any form will be of the past.

Words have a significant impact on where you end up. I am sure most people have words or phrases that have lodged in their minds from perhaps even years ago. Some, like the torment of hovering dark grey clouds, will be lies, but if they have stuck, they are likely to have had an adverse effect. Some will be beautiful, like a sunrise or sunset over a desert, and stay in your mind for you to revisit at any time.

Those words that my teacher said just before I left school, "You may as well jump off a bridge because you're going nowhere," were condemning and brutal, destructive, unnecessary – and an outrage. Lives are affected by words like this and they can make us lose hope. Many have gone astray, perhaps ending up on the streets or in prison, because at some point in their lives someone wasn't careful with their choice of words to them.

If you believe in your mind that something is possible or isn't possible and you speak it out, then it becomes what you decide: where the mind goes, the man follows. What you speak is what you become.

Words of Growth

Affirmations are enormously powerful, whether building a business, looking after your health, taking on a new job, or being a parent – in fact for anything that keeps your belief alive and motivates you to be to be the best you can. Words you say about yourself are more important than anything anyone else says about you or thinks of you.

Can you think of a time in your life when someone said something to you that helped you grow, that moved you forward and that had an impact on your direction? Words of encouragement allow us to stand tall, to motivate us to want to continue being our best, grow our self-worth and create in us a healthy spirit and desire for hard work.

If you use words well you can build bridges across incomprehension and chaos. Whatever your situation, wherever you are on your journey, note the importance of your words and the words you choose to listen to. Make a decision to ramp up positive words a gear. It will change the atmosphere in your home and create greater results in your workplace. It will sharpen your conscience and different things will start to matter and happen. You can jumpstart your day by thinking and speaking good things.

A quick exercise that will be valuable to you throughout your day if done at the start of it is to speak out positive statements like:

'Today I am energetic and creative.'

'I am thankful for today and that I can be a blessing to others.'

'My wings are stronger than the wind.'

'Today I can handle whatever comes my way.'

Your words are not the cause all of your problems, but they can create a lot of   them. They should be given a good deal of consideration when you use them but also when you are looking for answers in life.

How many bosses are hated because of how they make their staff feel? How many married people create enemies of each other because of mean and cruel words? How many businesses are ill reputed because of what people have heard their representatives say? Will they know peace at night? Perhaps those who speak so negatively believe it is worth it just for the control, but too late they will find out it is futile to the end.

How do you want people to remember you when you are gone? How would you like your eulogy to read?

'*They were such a kind person, always building up, never knocking down, encouraging and supportive to the end. Genuine to a tee and remarkable in their ability to run a massively successful business with not one enemy. Their words were so powerful and drove people to be their best because they constantly told them that they were the best.*'

It has been said that our eyes are windows to our soul and I believe that our words are also an indication of who and what we are inside. This is another reason why starting with your core is paramount to your journey, as this will have bearing on both your attitude, decisions, and language.

Almost every emotion we feel as a human being is affected or created by the words we hear or say. The very words we utter every day create the world we live in. They have the power to crush countries and the power to build nations anew. They *are* power. They can be your power to change a life, to inspire a nation, and make this world a beautiful place. One thing is for sure, speaking negatively could hurt and speaking positively never will, so why not go with the positive and see what results you get?

By changing your words, you could change your world.

Chapter 9 : Living Victoriously

Imagine you've just been told that you have two months to start living from your core, to start believing in who you are with an attitude of hopeful expectation, to start being passionate about what you do, and to take steps of faith which enable you to move into a life of victory. But if you don't, then at the end of those two months you will never have the opportunity again.

How motivated would that make you to do something about all that we have talked through?

Because this is the thing – you have to take action. Some will do this and live a great life; others will continue to live in a world of 'whatever happens'!

My children used to have a kaleidoscope. When you looked into it, the tiny, coloured pieces formed a picture. When you shook it, the same pieces would create a completely different picture every time.

Our lives are a bit like that kaleidoscope. Depending on the decisions we make, the way we go, the thoughts we allow ourselves to have, and the place we choose to come from, we create a picture which is our lives.

But this is your life and it's up to you to make decisions that create the picture you want.

You may have been through the darkest time you can imagine, but now it's time to start looking for the stars. It's time to shake off the past. Because if you spend today thinking and dwelling on yesterday's errors, or other people's mistakes, you'll never make the progress you desire because guilt, condemnation, and unforgiveness will steal your energy.

Lewis B. Smedes said, "To forgive is to set a prisoner free and discover that the prisoner was you."

Happiness is the Key

What seems an end is often a beginning and it's at this point that new life springs from wounds. It's time to wake up with new attitude and determination: to be excited about today, not exasperated. No longer living in denial but letting truth about who you are and what you can and will achieve be at the forefront of your mind every waking hour, taking the decision to conquer and be a champion.

Remind yourself that you are the only you there will ever be and that you are the only person on earth who will ever truly know everything about you. Now is the time to live how you were intended to. It is time to find those passions that have perhaps been with you all the time, just not fully realised, or forgotten.

Perhaps passions you never realised you had could trigger what comes next in your life. They are the ones you need to find. A person gets old when their regrets surpass their dreams. You'll never regret the things you try and fail at, you may regret the things you never try. Success is not the way to happiness: happiness is the key to success. If you love what you are doing, you will be successful.

To have the victory there has to be a struggle and you have to fight through. We often have to push through pain to get the results we desire. The fruit of sore struggle will come out of the frosts of autumn, the storms of winter, and the rains and sunshine of spring. Yours may be a story of conflict – with defeats, wounds, and tears – but this is your time now to change that.

What does living victoriously look like to you? What does it mean? I suggest that you reflect and write down your thoughts.

I believe a key part of living victoriously is having the mindset of a champion, standing tall with acceptance and humility. It's about paying attention to details, not trying to impress others who watch you without understanding you or where you're going. It's about deciding what journey you're on and implementing each stage of it. It's about being thankful for every day and acknowledging that each one is a gift.

Get used to smiling and laughing because there will be a lot of that on the other side of each door you go through, if at the start you make a concerted effort to practise each day. Smiles are infectious and magical and can be detected from the sound of your voice. So even on the phone the person listening to you is likely to pick up on your mood. Become known as the person who always smiles. People will be drawn to you.

Why should you do this? Because you no longer want to be robbed of time. This is the beginning of a new attitude, strength, determination, and excitement in all that is out there for you.

Doing Time

During my time going into prison I met men who were in for varied amounts of time, for every type of crime, from drink driving to murder. Some were 'lifers', in for a minimum of 20 years, and some were only there for weeks. I recall one Christmas I went in to help with the Boxing Day service, as it fell on a Sunday, and a guy I'd not seen before was there.

He was in a terrible state, wracked with sobs. I asked him if he was being bullied and he said he wasn't, so I did my best to calm him so I could ascertain the cause of his extreme stress. Having never been in trouble with the police before, he had been caught drink driving. He hadn't crashed or harmed anyone but, as they have the power to do, the courts decided to jail him for six weeks.

He was in shock, and although he had only been in so far for two weeks – which he said had felt like two years – he had lost his job as a Chartered Surveyor with a highly reputable organisation, his partner had walked out, and he was hanging on to life by worn-out threads. He had four weeks to go and he couldn't contain his anxiety. In a barely audible voice, he explained how the six weeks of 'robbed time' equated to all he'd ever worked for. There was such an urgency and desperation in his voice, and the turmoil inside him had created a sprung coil that was so tight that he almost needed restraining.

It was interesting to witness other men, however, who were in for much longer periods but mentally far less imprisoned than a large number of men I speak to on the outside. They had searched their core and started working from the inside out and were now making the best use of their time, and no longer being robbed of it.

As you make a decision to move from struggle to grace and into a life of victory, the compartments of your life will become uncluttered, opened, and aired. You will have to work hard and maintain a high standard of self-awareness. You will have to manage yourself enough to keep your thoughts and attitudes where they need to be in order to make yourself successful and fulfilled and remain in a place of contentment.

Joyce Meyer wrote, 'Once I realised that right thinking is vital to victorious living, I got more serious about thinking about what I was thinking about and choosing my thoughts carefully.'

Letting Go of Power

When coming from the 'outside in', one thing that I have seen many people hit walls over is power. Victory found in power is surface contentment: self-gratifying and short-lived. The eagle is a powerful bird which never flies from storms and has a conquering spirit. Soar like the eagle you are, but don't choose power over faith. Power isolates you. Don't be someone who closes the gates, pulls up the drawbridge, and keeps people out. Often behind the show of force and power, people fear that what they have accumulated may be taken from them.

Are you holding on to your power, afraid of anyone else getting hold of it or taking it away from you? If this is you, you may find places of contentment for a while and may even allow yourself to celebrate, but your feelings will be like a yo-yo, up and down, never around for long, as you question life, purpose, and worth all over again. You'll strive to hit yet another goal that will give you the satisfaction and results your soul is after... until you get there and find the boundaries have changed yet again.

This, as you know, is what happens when you put the petals before the bud, where you allow power and all that is outside you to make you who you are. It's a journey marked out for dissatisfaction and unrest. This power and fear of loss needs to be put to rest, laid down, and replaced by sharing, giving, and getting to where others are at.

To remain in a place of contentment and to start discovering inner peace, you will be aware of grime falling away from your 'snowball' as you become more whole. As you learn the art of true giving, the fear of losing and the need to hold on tight to everything will evaporate.

I am sure you remember doing 'join the dots' when you were a child or with your children. This is your join the dots… of you. Each step is one forward and if you are managing yourself well, it will be conducive to your purpose and life. When you allow yourself to live your way, rather than the way others think you should live, it changes everything.

By taking the lead in your own life you will find that it isn't only liberating, but you experience a freedom and a joy. It comes with responsibilities, too, in an outside world that can be very demanding, but the freedom and joy make the responsibility worthwhile.

This has to start with you getting yourself right with you.

I'll repeat my earlier question: on a scale of 1-10 – with 1 being bad and 10 being good – what do you think of yourself?

How much do you believe in and like or love yourself?

Life as a Gift

Sun Tzu said, "Victorious warriors win first and then go to war, while defeated warriors go to war first and then seek to win."

I am sure you know someone who once received the unexpected and horrific news that they had only months to live. Sometimes, when I am sitting in a place with people I don't know, a waiting room or an airport for example, I find myself looking around at them wondering about their lives. It always amazes me that although I am so close to them, I know nothing of the joy or trauma, devastation or exhilaration in their worlds. It makes me so thankful to sit and think in that moment that I am not, to my knowledge, living the last days or months of my life.

I don't have a ticking clock strapped to my wrist. It makes me breathe in life with a deeper gratitude and I urge you to do the same. We all have a limited time clock and it has to be your decision to live life each day as though it were the best yet because the truth is, you don't know when it will be your last.

At times you may be tempted to stay at home when faced with hard decisions, cocooned in the warmth and security of what you know, to turn back rather than look uncertainty right in the face. The world can seem so threatening, and changes so rapid, but it's important now to widen your horizons and with confidence explore the possibilities of life and love and you.

If you now see life as a gift, it is not an option to allow yourself to live a life of monotony or mere existence. What a waste that would be! It is time to grab life and make every day count.

Having travelled amongst different countries, cultures, and climates, I have found myself increasingly staggered by the beauty and diversity of our world, and it has changed me significantly. It's like a magical secret to know that much of creation will never be seen or experienced.

What we can experience, however, we need to soak up, and be influenced and touched by its variety and magnificence. Notice what's under your feet because nature will teach you so much if you allow it to.

Actions are a by-product of your thoughts. Once your thoughts are on the right track and you are ready and raring to go, it's OK to devote large amounts of energy to accomplishing a goal worth having. But be sure that you are going after the goal that aligns with who you are, your beliefs, your dreams, and your values because this is about you, your purpose, and your passion. When you think about this, what words come to mind?

Perhaps fulfilment, peace, joy, excitement, contentment, self-belief, and self-worth. These are all fantastic words to aspire to, and as long as they are coming from your core, then they will become part of the foundation on which you stand. This means that when challenges arise, which they will, you will be centred and stable, able to ride the storm and learn from them, not be crushed or destroyed by them.

Time to Play

A significant lesson I learned only in the last few years has been the art of celebration. I had honestly only ever thought one celebrated if a destination was reached or a goal achieved. Although once I left school I achieved a number of things, for the most part the applause was brief, and only if the target was reached or the bounty collected. It was actually my very good friends, Ben Leppier and Barry Davis, who taught me the importance of celebrating every little step forward.

Every good phone call, every potential deal or speaking opportunity, every new process logged or system understood. Every rectified computer issue or good staff meeting: *everything*. This of course doesn't mean spending lavishly every time but doing something for yourself that was an acknowledgement that you'd done well.

For me it was taking time to play the piano, to step out of the world of work and people for a couple of minutes and play something – anything – for me.

Many of your victories may be small wins that nobody sees but celebrate them. It will stand you in great stead when the going gets tough and for whatever reason you take a few steps back.

Remember not only to celebrate but to enjoy the little things in life. One day you'll look back and realise they were the big things.

I have a vivid memory from my time in the Kalahari in 1987. We were not on safari for a few days and we had been cleaning 'The Barren' – an old army truck with 16 gears and bench seating for 30 people. We had taken the canvas off the frame and, for some reason, I decided to attempt pull-ups on one of the top bars. Needless to say, I wasn't overly successful but I still remember the joy I felt that day, the freedom, the carefree state of mind in a place that had become my home.

It's a small memory but one I cherish, which has on many occasions pushed me on and made me smile. I believe that it was whilst I was in that place, experiencing the freedom to be myself, time to learn who I was and to take deep breaths of appreciation, that I became so aware that one life on this earth is all we get, whether it is enough or not. Surely, at the very least, we are mad if we don't live it as fully and bravely and beautifully as we can.

As you live one day at a time, making each day the best, you need to accept and expect imperfection – not only your own imperfection but that of others as well. Everyone has different strengths and weaknesses, and we all have issues. Instead of judging, learn *'to get to where they're at'*. This is crucial in your journey. Back in that waiting room or airport, watching the people with me, if I were to discover and write down the issues of every person in that place, they would probably amount to hundreds.

If it was possible to understand the pains created by those issues, the difficulties, the obstacles, the pressures, and the shocking paralysis that some cause, we may find ourselves far more sympathetic and ready to accept others' weaknesses where our worlds meet. This will make a daily difference to your relationships and your success in ironing out relational difficulties.

I listened to a story recently of a Thai lad who had become an orphan very young and been left to fend for himself, living on the streets for ten years and selling whatever he could in order to eat. He was discovered to have a truly beautiful voice and his determination and tenacity saw him passionately running after what he wanted. His situation and his issues (in his eyes) bore no relevance to the faith he had in his journey moving forward and he kept looking up as he made the decision to live out his purpose and passion. He was discovered and his voice has now been heard across the world. His resilience and determination was not shaken by his predicament.

You were born to win, overcome, and live in victory. Just like this boy, don't let a limited environment or something someone says stop you from being who you have been created to be. You know success is loving life, but you've got to dare to live it. You may not yet know what your passion or passions are but somewhere, something incredible is waiting to unfold and as part of your passion, perhaps you will be the person to discover it.

You have the opportunity to create revelations in the world of business of thought and of wisdom. I have found that faith may ask you to put some parts of life behind you and to move out without a detailed itinerary but when you get that whisper of peace that silences confusion a new strength surges up within you. There's an excitement and adventure about our unexpected journeys if we have the courage to stake the future on them.

As you live a life filled with both order and chaos, tears and laughter, strengths and weaknesses, remember when your body gets tired to let your mind say, 'This is where winners are made.'

Similarly, when your mind gets tired, let your heart say, 'This is where champions are made.'

Whatever and wherever you have come from, finding inner peace will make space for enjoyment and challenges, wisdom and growth.

It encompasses empathy and generosity, love and compassion and this now, is where you begin.

THE END

About the Author

Gillie is the founder of GMB Properties Ltd and a leading property expert in her field. Over the last 10 years she has been a mentor and coach and has developed her own specialist property courses.

In 1996 Gillie won the Childline Award for Great Britain, in 2011 she won a property Mastermind Course and in 2020 she won the WWA business woman of the year award.

Gillie is known as one of the UKs foremost authorities in the field of property education and creative programmes

Gillie currently lives in Oxfordshire, England with her 3 children.

Acknowledgments

I want to thank Mindy Gibbins-Klein for helping me to extract from my head and heart what needed to be said. Your method is amazing and I can't thank you enough.

Dave Guest for encouraging me to audio it myself and for always believing in the message I had for everyone

Liz Ford for lovingly listening to chapter after chapter in a tent one slightly wet summer.

And lastly Marcus Flynn for his patience, time, generosity, calming influence, expertise and phenomenal help, all of which meant an audio with me as the reader could be created.

People referred to in the Book

Henry Ford
Woody Allen
Jacquie Pullinger
Roger Bannister
Winston Churchill
Angelia Jolie
Nelson Mandela
Reinhold Niebuhr
Teddy Roosevelt
Lewis B. Smedes
Joyce Meyer
Sun Tzu

Printed in Great Britain
by Amazon

83572341R00066